**GREYSTONE'S Creative Hands**

**EDITOR**

Beverley Hilton

GREYSTONE PRESS/NEW YORK · TORONTO · LONDON

# Volume 18

# Contents

# sew easy

# beach or bathwear

Beach wrap, housecoat, or bathrobe/ lounge robe . . . choose the long or the short length, with sleeves or with the cool sleeveless look, in whatever fabric suits the purpose of the wrap. In printed terry cloth plus a matching turban it's an ideal outfit for a vacation.

## The wrap

### Fabrics and notions

For the long wrap you will need:
- [ ] $4\frac{1}{4}$ yds 36 inch wide fabric.
- [ ] $4\frac{1}{2}$ yds 1 inch wide folded braid

For the short wrap you will need:
- [ ] 3 yds 36 inch wide fabric.
- [ ] 4 yds 1 inch wide folded braid

For both lengths you will need:
- [ ] Graph paper for patterns
- [ ] $\frac{1}{2}$ inch wide seam tape or bias binding
- [ ] Matching thread

### The pattern

The pattern is for a 36 inch bust and 38 inch hip but can be adjusted to fit most figures with bust measurements between 34 and 38 inches.
Make back, front and sleeve patterns from those on graph. The squares on the graph represent 1 inch squares.

### Altering the size

**1a,b.** To increase or decrease the pattern width by 2 inches, cut both back and front down the dotted line and either spread (**a**) or overlap (**b**) by $\frac{1}{2}$ inch.

**1c, d.** To widen the sleeve, cut down the dotted line and spread 1 inch.
To enlarge the armhole to correspond cut across the dotted lines back and front and spread $\frac{1}{2}$ inch each.

### Cutting out

Lay out the pattern on the fabric as shown, noting that the back is cut on the fold of the fabric.
The pattern does not have seam or hem allowances; so add $\frac{1}{2}$ inch turnings on all seams, a 1 inch hem on the sleeves and a 2 inch hem around the bottom. Do not add turnings to the front and neck edges which are to be bound.

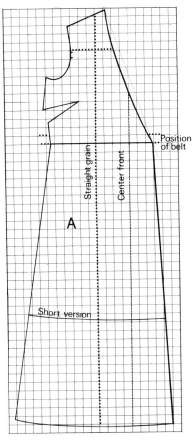
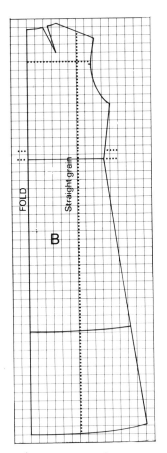

A

Straight grain

Center front

Position of belt

Short version

B

FOLD

Straight grain

*Above left: garment front. Above right: garment back. Below: sleeve*

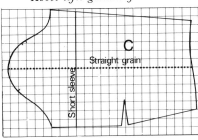

C

Straight grain

Short sleeve

Back views     Front views

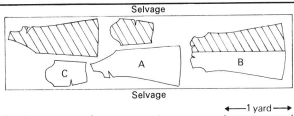

Selvage

C   A   B

Selvage

← 1 yard →

Layout of
the pattern
pieces for
the long
wrap

Layout of
the pattern
pieces for
the short
wrap

KEY
A = front
B = back
C = sleeve

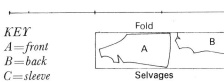

Fold

A   B   C

Selvages

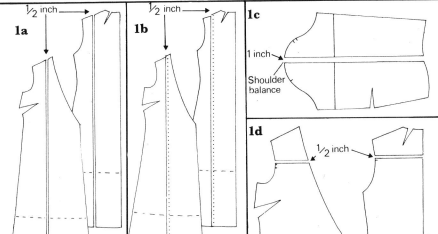

1a   ½ inch →

1b   ½ inch →

1c

1 inch

Shoulder
balance

1d   ½ inch →

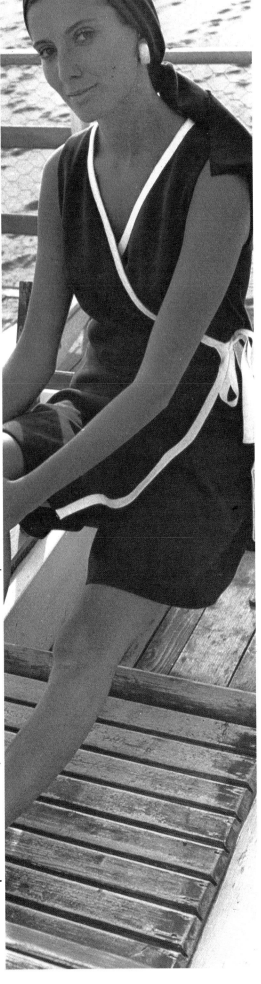

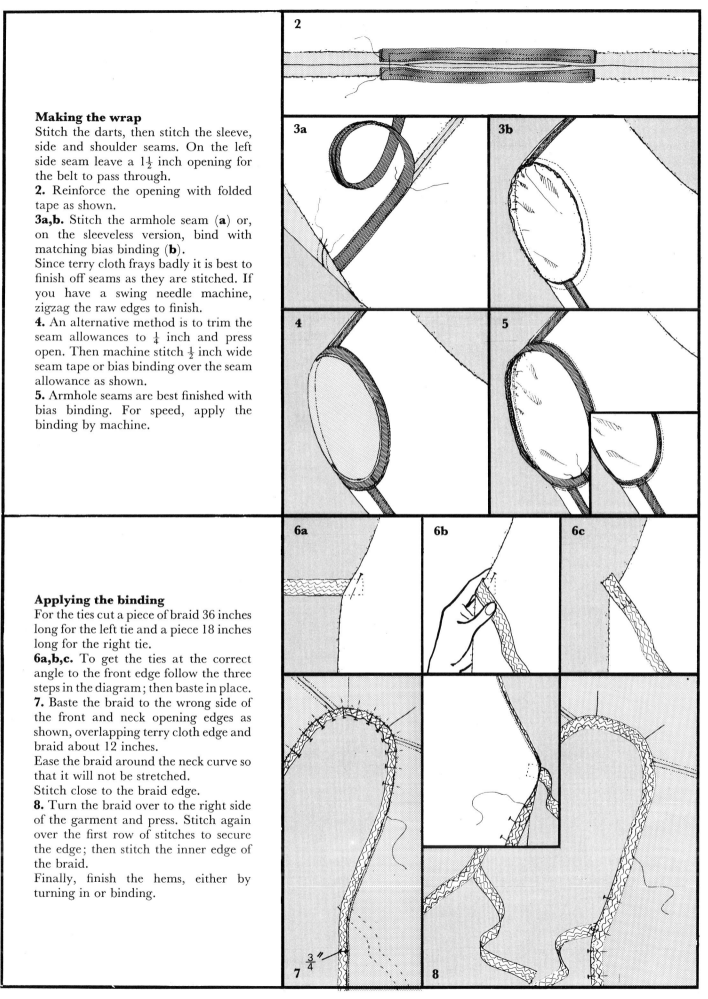

### Making the wrap

Stitch the darts, then stitch the sleeve, side and shoulder seams. On the left side seam leave a $1\frac{1}{2}$ inch opening for the belt to pass through.

**2.** Reinforce the opening with folded tape as shown.

**3a,b.** Stitch the armhole seam (**a**) or, on the sleeveless version, bind with matching bias binding (**b**).

Since terry cloth frays badly it is best to finish off seams as they are stitched. If you have a swing needle machine, zigzag the raw edges to finish.

**4.** An alternative method is to trim the seam allowances to $\frac{1}{4}$ inch and press open. Then machine stitch $\frac{1}{2}$ inch wide seam tape or bias binding over the seam allowance as shown.

**5.** Armhole seams are best finished with bias binding. For speed, apply the binding by machine.

### Applying the binding

For the ties cut a piece of braid 36 inches long for the left tie and a piece 18 inches long for the right tie.

**6a,b,c.** To get the ties at the correct angle to the front edge follow the three steps in the diagram; then baste in place.

**7.** Baste the braid to the wrong side of the front and neck opening edges as shown, overlapping terry cloth edge and braid about 12 inches.

Ease the braid around the neck curve so that it will not be stretched.

Stitch close to the braid edge.

**8.** Turn the braid over to the right side of the garment and press. Stitch again over the first row of stitches to secure the edge; then stitch the inner edge of the braid.

Finally, finish the hems, either by turning in or binding.

# Cross-stitch in fashion

A motif worked in a single stitch gives this peasant-style blouse its colorful appeal—and it's quite astonishing just how adaptable this kind of motif can be. It could be used for a linen tablecloth and matching napkins, a bedspread, sheets, dish towels, a curtain edging or even a hatband. The secret lies in deciding just how much of the motif can be used effectively.

## To work cross-stitch

For this type of embroidery on counted threads, it is important to maintain an even, regular appearance; for this reason, the upper half of all the stitches must lie in one direction. Cross-stitch may be worked from left to right or right to left, however, keeping this in mind.

For filling large areas of solid cross-stitch it is possible to work the first stitch of each cross in one direction and then return along the same row, completing each stitch. Although quicker than working one complete cross at a time, the results are less satisfactory. After working one row of cross-stitch, begin the next using the points at which the needle has moved in and out of the material for the first row. In this way, each row of stitches is immediately adjacent to the next.

## Embroidery on the blouse

The fabric for cross-stitch embroidery should be of even weave and depending upon the density of the material used, embroider with either four or six strands of floss in the needle. Cross-stitch can be worked on cotton, lawn, organdy, linen, or even-weave man-made fiber fabrics.

The following colors in D.M.C. 6-strand floss have been used for the blouse illustrated:

992 medium jade green
943 dark jade green
603 medium old rose
600 dark old rose
     black

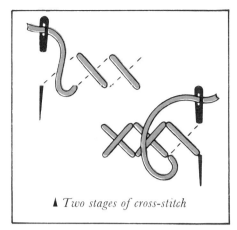

▲ *Two stages of cross-stitch*

## Ways with cross-stitch motifs

Work the entire motif in the center of a bright-colored linen tablecloth and repeat the border area around the edge of the cloth. Napkins might be in a contrasting color—perhaps gold napkins with a gray-green cloth, and with the embroidery worked in the same shades as on the tablecloth. Keep the embroidery on the napkins relatively simple; the stylized floral motif alone echoes the feeling of the larger piece. The motif could be repeated all over a bedspread or worked just across the top, with the border edging the entire piece. Try the motif in thick embroidery thread on coarsely woven linen. For a smaller piece of embroidery work the border pattern alone on a strip of vibrant-colored silk as a hatband . . . perfect trim for a large, floppy hat in felt or straw. Work the whole motif as a repeat around the edge of a full skirt or as a panel down the front of a dress. The single central flower motif could be embroidered on a knitted or crocheted sweater—or try the motif as a pattern for needlepoint enlarged for a brilliant pillow or on fine mesh canvas for a beautiful accessory.

▲ *One half of the motif as tracing pattern: embroidery worked on counted threads*

▲ *Adapting the motif—just a few possibilities*

1876

# stunning sunny time stripes

A sizzle of breathtaking stripes shown here in a combination of white, blue, green and orange makes this striking beach set. Halter topped, with a zipper fastened skirt, it is simple to make in rows of half double and is the sun seekers' answer to summer days. Use other colors if you wish.

## Sizes
**Halter top.** Directions are for 32in bust.
**Skirt.** Directions are for 34in hips.
Length, 22in.
The figures in brackets [] refer to the 34 and 36in bust sizes, and the 36 and 38in hip sizes respectively.

## Gauge
11 sts and 8 rows to 2in over hdc worked on No.D hook.

## Materials
Coats & Clark's O.N.T. Speed-Cro Sheen 100 yd. balls
6 [6:7] balls main color A
6 [6:6] balls contrast color B
3 [3:4] balls each of two contrast colors, C and D
One No. D (3.00 mm) crochet hook
Two buttons
22 in. open-ended zipper
Waist length elastic

## Skirt back

Using No.D hook and B, ch73[79:85] and beg at waist.
**1st row** Into 3rd ch from hook work 1hdc, work 1hdc into each ch to end. Turn. 71[77:83] sts.
**2nd row** Ch2 to count as first hdc, work 1 hdc into each st to end. Turn.
**3rd row** Attach A and work as 2nd row.
**4th row** Attach C and work as 2nd row.
**5th row** Attach D, ch2, 1hdc into next st, work 2hdc into next st, 1hdc into each of next 15[17:19] sts, work 2hdc in next st, 1hdc into each of next 33[35:37] sts, work 2hdc into next st, 1hdc into each of next 15[17:19] sts, work 2hdc into next st, 1hdc into each of next 2 sts. Turn. 75[81:87] sts.
Continue in hdc without shaping, working 2 rows A and 1 row B.
**9th row** Using B, ch2, 1hdc into next st, work 2hdc into next st, 1hdc into each of next 16[18:20] sts, work 2hdc into next st, 1hdc into each of next 35[37:39] sts, work 2hdc into next st, 1hdc into each of next 16[18:20] sts, work 2hdc into next st, 1hdc into each of next 2 sts. Turn. 79[85:91] sts.
Continue to work in striped patt of 1 row A, 1 row C, 1 row D, 2 rows A and 2 rows B, *at the same time*, inc as before on every 4th row 5 times more, then on every following 10th row until work measures 22in from beg, ending with 2 rows B. Fasten off.

## Skirt front

Work as given for Back.

## Halter top

Using No.D hook and B, ch135[139:143].
Work first 2 rows as given for Skirt back. 133[137:141] sts.
Continue in stripes, reversing order of colors given for Skirt and working 2 rows A, 1 row D, 1 row C, 1 row A and 2 rows B throughout.

### Shape top
**3rd row** Ch2, skip one st, 1hdc into each of next 46[47:48] sts, work 3hdc into next st, 1hdc into each of next 35[37:39] sts, work 3hdc into next st, 1hdc into each of next 40[41:42] sts, 1sc in next st. Turn.
**4th row** Ch2, skip one st, 1hdc into each of next 40[41:42] sts, work 3hdc into next st, 1hdc into each of next 37[39:41] sts, work 3hdc into next st, work in hdc to last 8 sts, 1sc in next st. Turn.
**5th row** Ch2, skip one st, 1hdc into each of next 40[41:42] sts, work 3hdc into next st, 1hdc into each of next 39[41:43] sts, work 3hdc into next st, work in hdc to last 8 sts, 1sc into next st. Turn.
Continue to inc in this way on next 5 rows, keeping inc sts in line, at the same time work one st less at beg and 7 sts less at end of these rows. 101[105:109] sts.
**Next row** Ch2, skip one st, patt to last 8 sts, 1sc into next st. Turn.
Rep last row 3 times more. 69[73:77] sts.
**Next row** Ch2, skip one st, patt to last 4[5:6] sts, 1sc into next st. Turn.
Rep last row 3 times more. 53 sts.
**Next row** Ch2, skip one st, patt to last 4 sts, 1sc into next st. Turn.
Rep last row 11 times more. Fasten off.

## Straps

Using No.D hook and B, ch138[143:148].
Work first row as given for Skirt back.
Continue in hdc, working 1 row A, 1 row D and 1 row C. Fasten off.
Make second strap in same manner.

## Finishing

**Skirt.** Press each piece under a damp cloth with a warm iron. Join right side seam. Sew zipper into left side seam with slide at bottom of skirt. Sew elastic at waist with casing-st. Press seam.
**Halter top.** Press as for Skirt. Sew on straps, beg at back and work around to point at top, leaving 8 inches of strap free for halter neck. Sew button onto one side of back and second button to end of one strap. Make button loops on other sides to correspond. Press seams.

▼ *Close-up showing the detail of the bust darts and halter neckline*

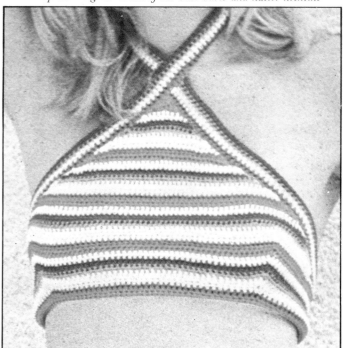

# Fringed belt-bag in macramé

A sophisticated macramé bag with a long silky fringe to slot casually on a wide belt for daytime wear, or to adapt for evening with a chain necklace threaded through the loops and held double.

## Size
Width, 7in
Length excluding fringe, 7in
Fringe, 9in

## Materials
Tubular rayon
200 yards pink
One 6in zipper
2 pieces of lining fabric, 7in by 7in
Matching sewing thread
One ready-made belt up to 2in wide

## Front

Cut twenty-three cords each nine feet long and one cord sixteen feet long.
Fold the sixteen-foot length so that one end is four and a half feet long and the other end eleven and a half feet long.
Knot all these cords doubled onto a holding cord, placing the long piece on the right-hand edge. Throughout the work this cord will act as leader for the horizontal knotting.
*Work two rows of horizontal knotting. Divide the cords into groups of four and work two square knots on each group. Work another two rows of horizontal knotting.
Divide the cords into groups of twelve and work a double diagonal cross as illustrated.
Repeat from * once more.

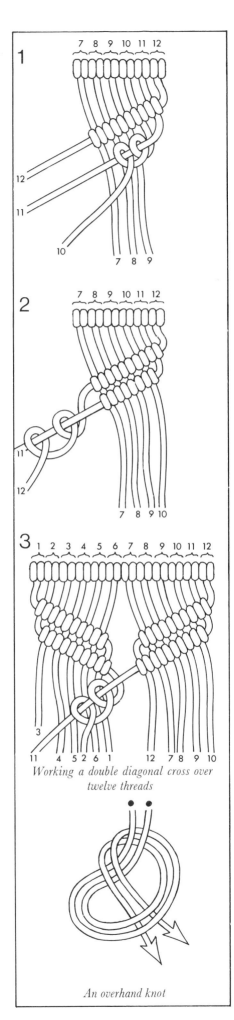

*Working a double diagonal cross over twelve threads*

*An overhand knot*

Work two rows of horizontal knotting. Divide the cords into groups of four. Work two square knots on each group. Work another two rows of horizontal knotting.
Divide the cords into groups of four. Starting from the left, work two square knots on each of the first two groups, three square knots on each of the next two groups, four square knots on the next group and five on the next. Reverse the sequence by working four square knots on the next group and so on, to end of the row.
Work two rows of horizontal knotting. Leave nine inches for the fringing and trim.

## Back

### Belt loops
Cut seven cords of ten feet each and one cord seventeen feet long.
Divide into groups of four (the group with the long cord should be level at one end, the longer piece hanging from the other end) and work four inches of square knots in the middle.
Fold each braid in half and knot onto the holding cord for the back with double basic cording knots as in horizontal knotting, positioning one braid at each end with the long cord on the right.
Cut sixteen cords nine feet long, double and knot onto the holding cord between the belt loops.
Complete the back as given for the front.

## Finishing

Lay the zipper flat and stitch the top edges of the lining fabric to either side, making half inch turnings.
Position fabric so that the zipper lies along the top, stitch around the edges of the lining leaving a half inch seam allowance and incorporating into it the ends of the zipper.
Fasten off all the ends of the macramé to the back of the work.
With zipper open, slip stitch lining to back of the first holding cord of the macramé, one side to the front piece, the other to the back piece.
With matching sewing thread, overcast the sides of the macramé bag on the right side. At the lower edge of the bag stab stitch between the last two rows of horizontal knotting, catching in the lining.
Fringing can be added to the lower bar of the belt buckle to give a matching look. Here, setting on knots have been used and secured with one overhand knot.

1879

1880

# Brilliant for a bathroom

This dazzling yet practical bathroom set is worked in nylonized yarn for easy washing and quick drying. The technique of working a basic mesh onto which is added a surface crochet gives an effective texture.

## Sizes

**Bath mat.** About 22in by 38in, excluding fringe.
**Pedestal mat.** About 22in by 29in, excluding fringe.

---
**Gauge**
4sp to 3in.

---

## Materials

Knitting Worsted (4 oz. skeins)
8 skeins White
6 skeins Orange
5 skeins Yellow
5 skeins Scarlet
One No. I (5.50 mm) crochet hook

## Bath mat

### Foundation

Using No. I hook and two strands white, ch 76.
**1st row** 1dc into 6th ch from hook, *ch1, skip next ch, dc in next ch, rep from * to end. Turn. 36 sp.
**2nd row** Ch 4, *1dc into next dc, ch1, rep from * to last sp, 1dc into 3rd of 4 ch. Turn.

Rep 2nd row 55 times more. Fasten off.

### Surface crochet

Using No.I hook and double yarn throughout, with RS facing work 3sc into each of 2 sides of each sp, working around the sts and not into them and progressing in a diagonal direction so that the work forms "steps" on the right side.
Work 3sc in same manner on 3 sides of the sp which comes at the apex of each zigzag. Begin working from right to left along the long side of the mat, beg with yellow and working 3sc over 9th dc from lower corner, turn the mat a quarter turn and work 3sc over the next side of the same sp. Turn the mat back to the first position and work 3sc over next dc up. Following the chart, continue in this manner until the entire surface of the mat is covered.

## Pedestal mat

### Foundation

Using No.I hook and white double, ch76.
Work as given for Bath mat but rep 2nd row 29 times.
**Next row** Patt over first 12sp. Turn.
**Next row** Skipping 4 turning ch, ss into next dc, ch4, patt to end. Turn.
**Next row** Patt to last dc. Turn.
**Next row** As for row before last. 9sp.
Continue without shaping on these sts for 13 rows more. Fasten off.
Attach yarn to 12th dc counting from other side, ch4, patt to end.
**Next row** Patt to last dc. Turn.
**Next row** Skipping 4 turning ch, ss into next dc, ch4, patt to end. Turn.
**Next row** Patt to last dc. Turn.
Complete this side to correspond to first. Fasten off.

### Surface crochet

Using No.I hook and double yarn throughout, work as given for Bath mat.

## Finishing

Pull all ends to the wrong side of the work and run in. Using No.I hook and white double, work 3sc into each sp all around outside edges. Ss to first sc. Fasten off.

### Fringe

**Bath mat.** Cut length of white about 4in long. Using 3 strands together and doubled, knot into every other sc all around outer edges.
**Pedestal mat.** Make fringe as for Bath mat, knotting into every other sc all around outside and top edges only.

*Chart showing the direction and patterning of the surface single crochet diamonds*

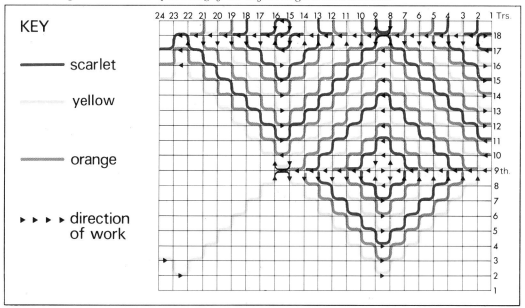

KEY
—— scarlet
...... yellow
—— orange
▶ ▶ ▶ ▶ direction of work

▼ *Detail of surface single crochet*

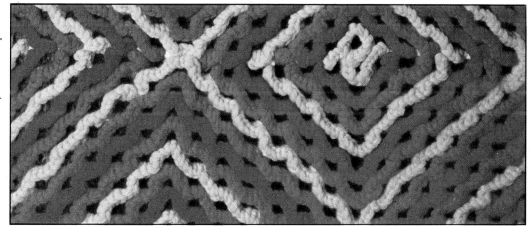

CROCHET

# For a fashion conscious baby

This charming little crochet pants suit for a baby has a top with sleeves, and straight pants.

To save any unnecessary finishing, the pants are worked in rounds, starting at the top and dividing for the legs which are then worked in individual rounds. Once completed, the elastic and braid have to be added. And, despite a slim fit, the open-work crochet of these pants has enough. give to pull over the bulk of baby's diapers.

**Sizes**

Directions are for 20in chest. The figures in brackets [] refer to the 22in size only.

**Top.** Length to shoulder, 10in. Sleeve seam, 1¾in.

**Pants.** Length from top to crotch, 6½in. Leg seam, 8in.

**Materials**
3-ply Baby Yarn
4 [5] ounces
One No. D (3.00 mm)
crochet hook
2 yd. braid
Waist length elastic
5 buttons

# Top bodice front

Using No.D hook, ch49[58].
**1st row** Into 2nd ch from
hook work 1hdc, 1hdc into
each ch to end. Turn.
**2nd row** Ch2, skip first hdc.
*1hdc in next hdc, rep from
* ending with 1hdc in top of
turning ch. Turn.
Rep 2nd row twice more.

**Shape armholes**
**1st row** Ss to 4th hdc, ch2,
1hdc into each hdc to last 3
sts. Turn.
**2nd row** Ch2, skip first hdc,
*1hdc in next hdc, rep from
* ending with 1hdc in top of
turning ch. Turn.
Rep 2nd row 8 times more.

**Shape neck and shoulders**
**Next row** Ch2, skip first
hdc, 1hdc into each of next
14[17] hdc. Turn.
**Next row** Dec one st, work
in hdc to end. Turn.
**Next row** Ss to 5th hdc, ch2
work in hdc to last st. skip
last st. Turn.
**Next row** Skip first st, work
in hdc to last 4 sts.
Fasten off.
With RS facing, skip first
12[14] sts, attach yarn to
13th [15th] st and complete
to correspond to first side,
reversing shapings.

# Top bodice right back

Using No.D hook, ch26[29].
**1st row** Into 2nd ch from
hook work 1hdc, 1hdc into
each ch to end. Turn. 25[28]
hdc.
**2nd row** Ch2, skip first hdc,
*1hdc into next hdc, rep
from * ending with 1hdc in

top of turning ch. Turn.
Rep 2nd row twice more.

**Shape armhole**
**Next row** Ss to 5th hdc, ch2,
*1hdc into next hdc, rep
from * ending with 1hdc in
top of turning ch. Turn.
Continue until work
measures same as Front to
shoulder, ending at armhole
edge.

**Shape shoulder**
**Next row** Ss to 5th [6th]
hdc, ch2, *1hdc into next
hdc, rep from * ending with
1hdc in turning ch. Turn.
**Next row** Ch2, skip first hdc,
*1hdc into next hdc, rep
from * to last 4[5] hdc. Turn.
**Next row** Ss to 5th [6th]
hdc, ch2, *1hdc into next
hdc, rep from * ending with
1hdc in top of turning ch.
Fasten off.

# Top bodice left back

Work as given for bodice
right back, reversing shaping.

# Top skirt

Join bodice seams.
Using No.D hook, attach
yarn to right Back bodice.
**1st row** Ch3, *skip 2 sts,
work 3dc, ch2, 3dc all into
next st, rep from * ending
with 1dc in last st. Turn.
**2nd row** Ch3, *work 3dc,
ch2, 3dc in ch2 sp, rep from *
ending with 1dc in top of
turning ch. Turn.
Rep 2nd row 12 times more.
Fasten off.

# Top sleeves

Using No.D hook, ch18.
**1st row** Into 5th ch from
hook work 2dc, ch1, work 2dc
in next ch, skip 3ch, *2dc,
ch1, 2dc all into next ch,
skip 3ch, rep from * once
more, 1dc in last ch. Turn.
**2nd row** Ch5, work 2dc, ch1,
2dc all into first dc, *work
2dc, ch1, 2dc all into next
ch1 sp, rep from * twice
more, work 2dc, ch1, 2dc
into 3rd of first 5ch. Turn.
**3rd row** Ch5, work 2dc, ch1,
2dc all into first dc, *work
2dc, ch1, 2dc all into next
ch1 sp, rep from * 4 times

more, work 2dc, ch1, 2dc
into 3rd of first 5ch. Turn.
**4th row** Ch5, work 2dc, ch1,
2dc all into first dc, *work
2dc, ch1, 2dc all into next
ch1 sp, rep from * 6 times
more, work 2dc, ch1, 2dc
into 3rd of first 5ch. Turn.
**5th row** Ch3, *work 2dc, ch1,
2dc all into next ch1 sp, rep
from * ending with 1dc into
3rd of first 5ch. Turn.
**6th row** As 5th row, but ending with 1dc into top of first 3ch.
Rep 6th row 4 times more.
Fasten off.

# Pants

Using No.D hook,
ch92[104] and beg at waist.
Join with a ss into first ch to
form a circle.
**1st round** Ch1 to count as
first sc, skip 1ch, work 1sc
into each ch to end. Join
with a ss into first ch.
Work 4 more rounds sc.
**6th round** Ch3, work 1dc,
ch1, 2dc all into first sc, skip
3sc, *work 2dc, ch1, 2dc all
into next sc, skip 3sc, rep
from * to end of round.
Join with ss to top of 3ch, ss
into ch1 sp in between dc. 24
[26] shells.
**7th round** Ch3, work 1dc,
ch1, 2dc into ch1 sp, *work
2dc, ch1, 2dc all into next
ch1 sp, rep from * to end of
round. Join with ss into top
of 3ch, ss into ch1 sp between.
**8th round** Ch3, work 1dc,
ch1, 2dc all into ch1 sp,
*work 2dc, ch1, 2dc all into
next ch1 sp, rep from * to
end of round. Join with a ss
into ch1 sp.
Rep 8th round 10 times more.
**Next round** Work as given
for 8th round, making shells
with 3dc, ch2 and 3dc.
Rep last round once more.

**First leg**
**Next round** Patt 6[7]
shells, work 3dc into next
shell, ch2, skip 11 [12]
shells, work 3dc into next
shell, continue in patt to end.
Join with a ss into ch2 sp.
**Next round** Work in patt to
3dc, skip 3dc, work 3dc into
first of 2ch, ch2, work 3dc
into 2nd of 2ch, skip 3dc,
patt to end. Join with a ss
into ch2 sp.

Continue in patt over sts of
first leg until work measures
8in from beg of leg.
Fasten off.

**Second leg**
Attach yarn to 6th [7th]
complete shell away from
division for legs, work in patt
to division for legs, work 3dc
into same sp as 3dc for first
leg, ch2, work 1sc into top
of first dc of 3dc for first
leg, work 3dc into first of 2ch,
ch2, work 3dc into 2nd of
2ch, work 1sc into top of
3rd dc of 3dc for first leg,
ch2, work 3dc in same sp
as 3dc for first leg, patt to
end. Join with ss to ch2 sp.

**Next round** Work in patt to
3dc, skip 3dc, work 1sc in 2ch,
1 shell in ch2 sp, work 1sc
in next 2ch, skip 3dc, 1
shell in next ch2 sp, patt to
end. Join with ss to ch2 sp.
Complete to match first leg.
Fasten off.

# Finishing

DO NOT PRESS.
**Top.** Join shoulders. Join
sleeves up to 6th patt row,
then set cap of sleeves into
armholes. Join back seam of
skirt. Mark positions for 5
buttons on left side of bodice.
**Edging.** Using No.D
hook, beg at bottom of left
side of Back and work 1 row
sc up left back, around neck
and down right back,
working 2sc in corners.
Turn. Work another row sc
around edges, dec one sc
over shoulder seams and in
corners of neckline. Turn.
Work another row sc around
edges, working 2sc in each
sc at corners and making 5
buttonholes on right side of
Back as markers are reached
by skipping 1sc and working
ch1. Sew on buttons. Sew
braid on bodice, beg level
with armholes, across bodice
on Back opening, along
sleeve, across bodice on front,
along sleeve and across other
half of back.
**Pants.** Run in ends.
Sew braid on 3rd round from
lower edge of each leg.
Sew elastic inside waist edge
using casing-st.

# Serpentine stitchery

Inspired by a floral form, the designer of this needlepoint panel has moved from the natural to the abstract, using embroidery silks, wools, metal threads and beads for a striking composition of textures. The subtle coloring of the panel doesn't seem to subdue the fluid, swirling shape; only the tips of the stamen attract attention for their own vividness. Suitable for a wall panel or a special pillow, the design might be elongated to cover a footstool or repeated for a smart, contemporary rug.

## Floral panel

The materials given here are for working the panel in the colors and stitches shown; the completed panel is 18 inches by 24 inches. To work this pattern on a larger piece of canvas for a stool or rug, increase the quantities of materials needed proportionately.

## Materials you will need

☐ ⅝yd of 27 inch wide canvas (16 single threads to 1 inch)
☐ 1 skein D.M.C. Tapestry yarn in each of the following colors—☐ Green 7396 ☐ dark green 7347 ☐ green 7342 ☐ yellow green 7548 ☐ dark blue 7319 ☐ blue 7307 ☐ blue 7304 ☐ light blue 7302 ☐ fawn 7124 ☐ orange 7852 ☐ red 7137
☐ 3 skeins D.M.C. Tapestry yarn in black
☐ 23 skeins D.M.C. Tapestry yarn in white
☐ 40 skeins of twisted embroidery silk in white or D.M.C. 6-strand floss in white (if D.M.C. floss is used, four strands in the needle are suggested)
☐ 1 skein of silver thread
☐ Black and silver bugle beads

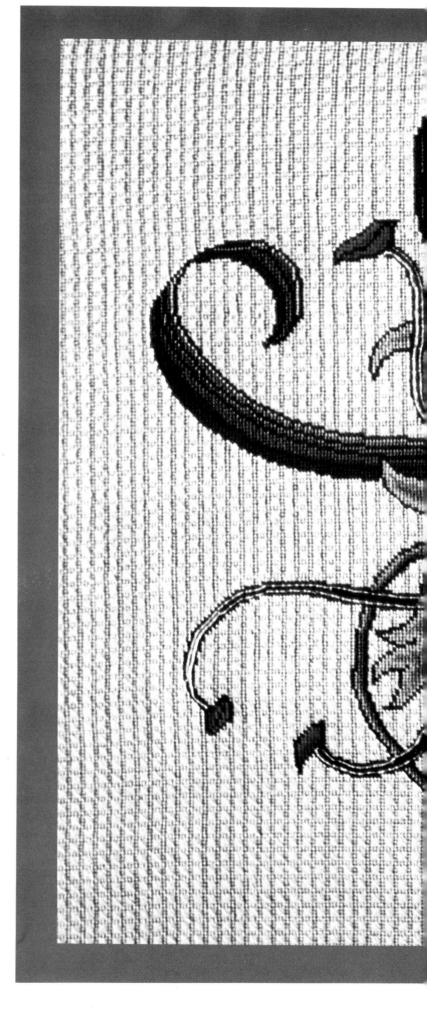

## Variations on the panel

If desired, alternate colors and stitches may be substituted for those previously given. A range of rusts and yellows would be effective against a white background, worked in a slightly more complex selection of stitches.

### Materials you will need

Make the following substitutions for the second, sixth and seventh items listed previously:

☐ 1 skein D.M.C. Tapestry yarn in each of the following colors—☐ Dark brown 7467 ☐ dark rust 7449 ☐ rust 7445 gold 7437 ☐ mustard brown 7508 ☐ olive brown 7485 ☐ yellow olive 7484 ☐ pale olive 7745 ☐ aquamarine 7909 ☐ aquamarine 7956

☐ Goldfingering in gold or bronze

### To work the alternative panel

For this panel, the flower is worked in a range of yellows, the leaves in rust and brown, and the contrasting accent of color remains, the tips of the stamen, this time worked in two shades of aquamarine.

The background is rice stitch, with alternating rows of white yarn worked with the corners crossed with goldfingering over four threads, and the reverse of this.

Work the flower in a small diagonal stitch, the leaves and stem in mosaic stitch; both of these stitches are good for indicating shaded areas. The stamen are worked in Smyrna stitch, using goldfingering (in either a gold or bronze color) over two threads.

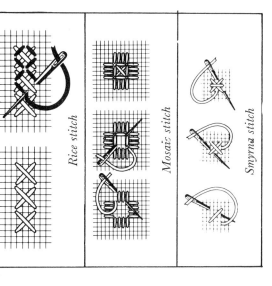

*Cushion stitch*

*Rice stitch*

*Mosaic stitch*

*Smyrna stitch*

### To work the panel

Only two stitches are used for this panel. The motif is worked entirely in tent stitch, and the background in cushion stitch with white yarn for the cushion shapes and twisted embroidery silk for the surrounding areas of tent stitch.

*Method of working tent stitch vertically, horizontally and diagonally*

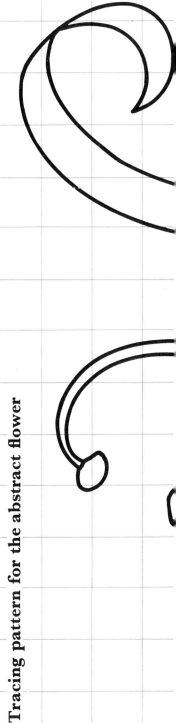

## Tracing pattern for the abstract flower

Each square = 1in

1887

# Blazoned with butterflies

Bright days for 9-12 year-olds in this twin set embroidered with butterfly motifs. The pullover and cardigan are worked first and the butterflies added in duplicate stitch over stockinette stitch.

## Sizes

Directions are for 28in chest. The figures in brackets [] refer to the 30 and 32in sizes respectively.
**Pullover.** Length to shoulder, 17½[19:20½]in.
Sleeve seam, 2½in.
**Cardigan.** Length to shoulder, 18[19½:21]in.
Sleeve seam, 12½[14:15½]in.

> **Gauge**
> 7 sts and 9 rows to 1in over st st worked on No. 3 needles.

## Materials

3-ply Fingering Yarn
1 oz. balls
**Pullover.** 5 [6:7] balls main color, A
**Cardigan.** 7 [8:8] balls main color, A
1 ball each of contrast colors, B and C, for embroidery
One pair No. 2 needles (or Canadian No. 11)
One pair No. 3 needles (or Canadian No. 10)
One 5 in. zipper for pullover
6 [6:7] buttons for cardigan

## Pullover back

Using No.2 needles and A, cast on 97[105:113] sts.
**1st row** K1, *P1, K1, rep from * to end.
**2nd row** P1, *K1, P1, rep from * to end.
Rep these 2 rows for 1½ in, ending with a 2nd row.

Change to No.3 needles. Beg with a K row, continue in st st, inc one st at each end of every 24th row until there are 103[111:119] sts.
Continue without shaping until work measures 11½ [12½:13½]in from beg, ending with a P row.

### Shape armholes

Bind off 3[4:5] sts at beg of next 2 rows and 2 sts at beg of next 4[4:6] rows.
Dec one st at each end every other row 2[3:2] times. 85[89:93] sts.
Continue without shaping until armholes measure 1½[2:2½] in, ending with a K row.

### Divide for back opening

**Next row** P40[42:44], K2, K2 tog, K1, P to end.
**Next row** K42[44:46], turn and slip rem sts on holder.
**Next row** K2, P to end.
Keeping 2 sts at inside edge in garter st, continue in st st until armhole measures 6[6½:7]in from beg, ending with a WS row.

### Shape shoulder and neck

Bind off at arm edge every other row 3 sts once, 3[3:4] sts once and 3[4:4] sts once, ending at neck edge.
Bind off 5[6:7] sts at neck edge at beg of next row.
Bind off 4 sts at beg of next 6 rows.
Bind off rem 4 sts.
With RS facing, attach yarn to rem sts and K to end.
**Next row** P to last 2 sts, K2.
Complete to correspond to first side, reversing shaping.

## Pullover front

Using No.2 needles and A, cast on 97[105:113] sts.

Change to No.3 needles. Beg with a K row, continue in st st, inc one st at each end of every 24th row until there are 103[111:119] sts.
Continue without shaping until work measures 11½ [12½:13½]in from beg, ending with a P row.

### Shape armholes

Bind off 3[4:5] sts at beg of next 2 rows and 2 sts at beg of next 4[4:6] rows.
Dec one st at each end every other row 2[3:2] times. 85[89:93] sts.
Continue without shaping until armholes measure 1½[2:2½] in, ending with a K row.

Work 1½in rib as given for Back, ending with a 2nd row.
Change to No.3 needles.
Commence front panel patt.
**1st row** K38[42:46], P1, K1, P1, K15, P1, K1, P1, K to end.
**2nd row** P39 43:47], K1, P17, K1, P to end.
Keeping center panel correct, work as given for Back until armhole shaping is completed.
Continue without shaping until armholes measure 4½[5:5½]in from beg, ending with a WS row.

### Shape neck

**Next row** Patt 37[38:39], bind off 11[13:15] sts, patt to end.
Complete this side first.
Work 1 row, then bind off at beg of next and every other row 3 sts once, 2 sts 3 times and one st 3 times.
Continue without shaping until armhole measures same as Back to shoulder, ending with a RS row.

### Shape shoulder

Bind off at arm edge every other row 3 sts 3[2:1] times and 4 sts 4[5:6] times.
With WS facing, attach yarn to rem sts and complete to correspond to first side, reversing shaping.

## Sleeves

Using No.2 needles and A, cast on 65[71:77] sts.
Work ¾in rib as given for Back, ending with a 2nd row and inc 9 sts evenly across last row. 74[80:86] sts.
Change to No.3 needles. Beg with a K row, continue in st st until work measures 2½in from beg, ending with a P row.

### Shape cap

Bind off 3 sts at beg of next 4 rows and 2 sts at beg of next 6 rows.
Dec one st at each end every other row 14[16:18] times, ending with a P row.
Bind off 2 sts at beg of next 6 rows. Bind off rem 10[12:14] sts.

## Neckband

Join shoulder seams. Using No.2 needles, A and with RS facing, pick up and K101 [105:111] sts around neck.
Keeping 2 sts at each end in garter st, work ¾in K1, P1 rib. Bind off in rib.

## Cardigan back

Using No.2 needles and A, cast on 99[107:115] sts.
Work 1½in rib as given for Pullover back, ending with a 2nd row.
Change to No.3 needles. Beg with a K row, continue in st st, inc one st at each end of every 24th row until there are 105[113:121] sts.
Continue without shaping until work measures 11¾ [12¾:13¾]in from beg, ending with a P row.

### Shape armholes

Bind off 3[4:5] sts at beg of next 2 rows and 2 sts at beg of next 4 rows.
Dec one st at each end every other row 3 times. 85[91:97] sts.
Continue without shaping until armholes measure 6¼[6¾:7¼]in from beg, ending with a P row.

### Shape shoulders and neck

Bind off 3[4:5] sts at beg of next 4 rows and 4 sts at beg of next 2 rows.
**Next row** Bind off 4 sts, K24, bind off 9[11:13] sts, K to end.
Complete this side first.
Bind off 4 sts at beg of next 6 rows, then bind off rem 4 sts.
With WS of work facing, attach yarn to rem sts and complete to correspond to first side, reversing shaping.

## Cardigan left front

Using No.2 needles and A, cast on 73[75:79] sts.
Work 1½in rib as given for Back, ending with a 2nd row and inc one st at end of last row on 30in size only.
73[76:79] sts.
Change to No.3 needles.
Commence panel patt.
**1st row** *K15[16:17], P1,

1889

*Blue butterflies on red*

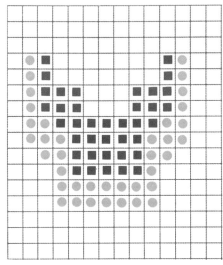

*Chart for the butterfly motif*

*Close-up detail of the butterfly*

K1, P1, rep from * twice
more, K19.

**2nd row** K1, P18, *P1, K1,
P16[17:18], rep from * twice.
Continue in patt inc one st
at beg of every 24th row
until there are 76[79:82] sts.
Continue without shaping
until work measures same as
Back to underarm, ending
with a WS row.

**Shape armhole**
Bind off at arm edge every
other row 3[4:5] sts once,
3 sts once, 2 sts 3 times and
one st 3 times. 61[63:65] sts.
Continue without shaping
until armhole measures
4½[5:5½] in from beg, ending
with a RS row.

**Shape neck and shoulder**
Bind off at beg of next and
every other row 19 sts once,
4 sts once, 3 sts once, 2 sts
3 times and one st 3 times,
*at the same time*, when armhole
measures same as Back to
shoulder, bind off at arm
edge every other row 3[4:5]
sts twice and 4 sts 5 times.
Mark positions for 6[6:7]
buttons on left Front, first to
come in center of lower
edging and last one in neckband, ⅝in above sts bound-
off at neck, with 4[5:5] more
evenly spaced between.

## Cardigan right front

Using No.2 needles and A,
cast on 73[75:79] sts.
Work ¾in rib as given for
Back, ending with a WS row.
**Next row** (buttonhole row)

Rib 4 sts, bind off 3 sts, rib
6 sts, bind off 3 sts, rib to
end.
**Next row** Rib to end,
casting on 3 sts above those
bound-off on previous row.
Continue in rib until work
measures 1½in from beg,
ending with a 2nd row and
inc one st at beg of last row
on 30in size only. 73[76:79]
sts.
Change to No.3 needles.
Commence panel patt.
**1st row** K19, *P1, K1, P1,
K15[16:17], rep from * twice
more.
**2nd row** P16[17:18], K1,
*P17[18:19], K1, rep from *
once more, P to last st, K1.
Complete to correspond to
left Front, reversing shaping
and working buttonholes as
before as markers are reached.

## Sleeves

Using No.2 needles and A,
cast on 53[57:61] sts.
Work 2½in rib as given for
Back, ending with a 2nd
row and inc 5[7:9] sts
evenly across last row.
58[64:70] sts.
Change to No.3 needles.
Beg with a K row, continue
in st st, inc one st at each
end of 7th and every
following 8th row until there
are 76[84:92] sts.
Continue without shaping
until sleeve measures
12½[14:15½]in from beg,
ending with a P row.

**Shape cap**
Bind off 3[4:5] sts at beg

of next 2 rows and 2 sts
at beg of next 6[8:10] rows.
Dec one st at each end
every other row 15 times,
ending with a P row.
Bind off 2 sts at beg of next 6
rows and 3 sts at beg of
next 2 rows. Bind off rem
10[12:14] sts.

## Neckband

Join shoulder seams. Using
No.2 needles and A, with RS
facing, pick up and K131
[135:139] sts around neck.
Work 1¼in K1, P1 rib,
working a pair of buttonholes
as before after ⅝in.
Bind off in rib.

## Finishing

**Pullover.** Press each piece
under a damp cloth with a
warm iron.
Sew in sleeves. Join side and
sleeve seams. Sew in zipper.
Press seams.
Working from chart with B
and C, embroider butterflies
on Front in duplicate stitch,
working a line of straight
stitches up center for body
and for antennae. Press.
**Cardigan.** Press as given for
Pullover.
Sew in sleeves. Join side and
sleeve seam. Fold front
bands in half to WS and slip
stitch in place.
Buttonhole-st around
buttonholes.
Embroider a butterfly in
each front panel, just above
edging, as for Pullover.
Press seams. Sew on buttons.

## Duplicate stitch

Rather than slow down the
process of knitting by adding
a colored motif into the
pattern, it is far quicker to
work the garment in stockinette stitch and then add the
motif in duplicate stitch.
This is done by outlining
the stitches of the motif area.
Thread the contrast yarn
into a darning needle and
pass the needle through to
the right side of the work
at the base of a stitch. Draw
the yarn through, leaving a
short end at the back to
run in once the work is
completed. Insert the needle
behind the threads at the
top of the same stitch, taking
the needle through to the
wrong side at the right-hand
side of the stitch and out to
the right side of the work at
the left of the stitch.
Next, insert the needle back

*Diagram showing how to work
Duplicate stitch*

into the base of the same
stitch. This has now outlined
one complete stitch and the
process is repeated over all
the necessary stitches. Run
in both ends invisibly on the
wrong side.

# Tatting bookmark

A gentle reminder to keep your place – a tatted bookmark. It can be made wider or longer and would make a beautiful gift for anyone who enjoys reading.

**Double stitch.** Hold end of thread in left hand to form ring. Lay shuttle thread in loop over ring and pass shuttle from underneath upward through ring and loop, right to left. Jerk shuttle thread to right so that knot transfers from being formed by the shuttle thread to being formed by the ring thread.
Next pass the shuttle through ring and loop downward from the top and jerk.
**Picots.** A picot is formed by leaving a gap between two double stitches and then closing them up.
**Chains.** To make a chain a second thread is introduced to make the knots and the original thread runs through as a core.
**Joining rings.** To join to a picot the second ring of thread is pulled through the picot by a small crochet hook and forms the first half of the next stitch. Complete the stitch in the usual manner and continue the work.

## Bookmark

### Size
6in by 1¾in, excluding fringes.

### Materials
Coats & Clark's Tatting Crochet No.70
(2) tatting shuttle(s)
**NB** This design can be worked with one shuttle and a ball thread if preferred

**Abbreviations**
ds = double stitch
p = picot
r(s) = ring(s)
ch = chain
sp = space

**1st row** R of 7ds, 1p, 7ds, close. Reverse work.
Ch of 7ds, 1p, 7ds. Reverse work.
R of 7ds, join to p of first r, 7ds, close. Reverse work.
*R of 7ds, 1p, 7ds, close. Reverse work.
Ch of 7ds, 1p, 7ds. Reverse work.
R of 7ds, join to p of last r, 7ds, close. Reverse work.
Repeat from * 13 times more, or for length required and making the total number of ch worked an uneven number.
Turn the row with r of 7ds, 1p, 7ds, close. Reverse work.
Ch of 7ds, 1p, 11ds. Reverse work.
R of 7ds, join to p of last r, 7ds, close. Reverse work.
Ch of 11ds, 1p, 7ds. Reverse work.
R of 7ds, join to previous

pair of rs, 7ds, close. Reverse work.
**2nd row** *R of 7ds, 1p, 7ds, close. Reverse work.
Ch of 7ds, join to p of opposite ch of previous row, 7ds. Reverse work.
R of 7ds, join to p of last r, 7ds, close. Reverse work.
R of 7ds, join to opposite pair of rs of previous row, 7ds, close. Reverse work.
Ch of 7ds, 1p, 7ds. Reverse work.
R of 7ds, join to group of 3rs, 7ds, close. Reverse work.
Repeat from * all along, turning the end of the row as before and joining the first turning ch to the opposite ch on previous row.
**3rd and 4th rows** As 2nd, finishing the end of the 4th row to match the beginning of the first row.

### Fringe
Cut 6 lengths of thread, each 6in long for each tassel and knot 4 tassels at each end of the bookmark as illustrated.

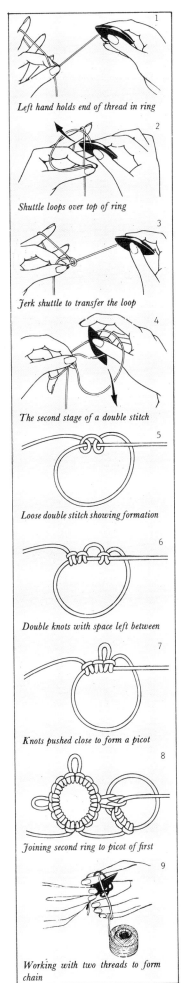

Left hand holds end of thread in ring

Shuttle loops over top of ring

Jerk shuttle to transfer the loop

The second stage of a double stitch

Loose double stitch showing formation

Double knots with space left between

Knots pushed close to form a picot

Joining second ring to picot of first

Working with two threads to form chain

# KNITTING

# Matched set

Matched-up cardigans in a simple "window pane" stitch – one buttoned to the neck, one with a V neckline.

## Sizes

Directions are for 34/36in bust/chest.
The figures in brackets [ ] refer to the 40/42in size only.
Length to shoulder, 24 [23]in.
Sleeve seam, 17½ [18½]in.

### Gauge
6 sts and 8 rows to 1in over st st worked on No. 6 needles.

## Materials

Reynolds Versaille
9 [10] 50 grm. balls
One pair No. 4 needles
(or Canadian No. 9)
One pair No. 6 needles
(or Canadian No. 7)
One No. 4 circular knitting needle
3 [5] buttons

## Back

Using No.4 needles, cast on 113 [129] sts.
**1st row** K1, *P1, K1, rep from * to end.
**2nd Row** P1, *K1, P1, rep from * to end.
Rep these 2 rows 4 [7] times more.
Change to No.6 needles. Commence patt.
**1st–7th rows** K.
**8th row** (WS) P7 [0], *K3, P13 [18], rep from * 5 times more, K3, P7 [0].
**9th row** K.
Rep 8th and 9th rows 6 [9] times more, then 8th row once. These 22 [28] rows form patt.
Continue in patt until work measures 17 [15]in from beg, ending with a WS row.

## Shape armholes

Keeping patt correct, bind off 4 sts at beg of next 2 rows

and 2 sts at beg of next 4 [6] rows.
K2 tog at each end every other row 4 [6] times.
89 [97] sts.
Continue without shaping until armholes measure 7 [8] in from beg, ending with a WS row.

## Shape shoulders

Bind off 5 [6] sts at beg of next 6 rows and 6 sts at beg of next 4 rows.
Slip rem 35 [37] sts on holder for back neck.

## Left front

Using No.4 needles, cast on 56 [64] sts.
**1st row** *K1, P1, rep from * to end.
Rep this row 9 [15] times more.
Change to No.6 needles. Commence patt.
**1st–7th rows** K.
**8th row** (WS) K1, *P13 [18], K3, rep from * twice more, P7 [0].
**9th row** K.
Rep 8th and 9th rows 6 [9] times more, then 8th row once.

## Woman's cardigan only

Continue in patt until work measures 13in from beg, ending with a WS row.

### Shape front
**Next row** Patt to last 3 sts, K2 tog, K1.
Work 3 rows without shaping.
Continue to dec in this manner on next and every foll 4th row until work measures same as Back to underarm, ending with a WS row.

### Shape armhole
Continue to dec at front edge as before on every 4th row, *at the same time*, bind off 4 sts at beg of next row and 2 sts every other row twice.
Dec one st at armhole edge every other row 4 times.
Continue to dec at front edge only until 27 sts rem.
Continue without shaping until armhole measures same as Back to shoulder, ending with a WS row.

### Shape shoulder
At arm edge, bind off every

other row 5 sts 3 times and 6 sts twice.

## Man's cardigan only

Continue in patt until work measures same as Back to underarm, ending with a WS row.

### Shape armhole
At arm edge, bind off every other row 4 sts once and 2 sts 3 times.
Dec one st at armhole edge every other row 6 times.
Continue without shaping until armhole measures 5in from beg, ending with a RS row.

### Shape neck
At neck edge, bind off every other row 3 sts twice and 2 sts twice.
K2 tog at neck edge every other row 8 times.
Continue without shaping until armhole measures same as Back to shoulder, ending with a WS row.

### Shape shoulder
At arm edge, bind off every other row 6 sts 4 times.

## Right front

Using No.4 needles, cast on 56 [64] sts.
**1st row** *P1, K1, rep from * to end.
Rep this row 9 [15] times more.
Change to No.6 needles. Commence patt.
**1st–7th rows** K.
**8th row** (WS) P7 [0], *K3, P13 [18], rep from * twice more, K1.
**9th row** K.
Rep 8th and 9th rows 6 [9] times more, then 8th row once.
Complete to correspond to left front, reversing shaping.

## Sleeves

Using No.4 needles, cast on 47 [55] sts.
Work 10 [16] rows rib as given for Back, inc 6 [1] sts evenly across last row. 53 [56] sts.
Change to No.6 needles. Commence patt.

## Woman's cardigan only

**Next row** K.
**Next row** P9, (K3, P13) twice, K3, P9.
Rep these 2 rows once more.

## Both versions

K7 rows.
**Next row** P9 [16], *K3, P13 [18], rep from * 1 [0] times more, K3, P9 [16].
Continue in patt as established to correspond to Back, inc one st each end every 10th

▲ *Detail of window pane patterning*

[8th] row until there are 75 [88] sts.
Continue without shaping until sleeve measures 17½ [18½]in from beg, ending with same patt row as for Back armhole.

## Shape cap

Bind off 4 sts at beg of next 2 rows and 2 [3] sts at beg of next 6 [2] rows.
(Bind off one st at beg of next 2 rows, then 2 sts at beg of next 2 rows) 7 times.
Bind off 2 sts at beg of next 4 [12] rows.
Bind off rem 5 [8] sts.

## Woman's front band

Using No.4 circular needle and RS facing, pick up and K 100 sts along right front to beg of shaping, 75 sts to neck, K across back neck sts, pick up and K 175 sts down left front edge. Join. 385 sts.
Beg with 2nd row of rib as given for Back, work 3 rows rib.
**Next row** (buttonhole row)

▲ *Two cardigans, in a matching stitch for a similar look, with their own distinctive design features*

Rib 9, (bind off 3, rib 39) 3 times, rib to end.

**Next row** Rib to end, casting on 3 sts above those bound off on previous row.
Rib 4 rows. Bind off in rib.

## Man's front band

Using No.4 circular needle and RS facing, pick up and K 152 sts along right front edge to neck, pick up and K 115 sts around neck including back neck sts on holder, and pick up and K 152 sts along left front edge. Join. 419 sts. Mark corner st at each side of front neck with thread. Beg with a 2nd row of rib as for Back, work 5 rows rib, inc one st at each side of corner sts on first and every other row.

**Next row** (buttonhole row) Rib to last 151 sts, (bind off 3, rib 31) 4 times, bind off 3, rib to end.

**Next row** Rib to end, casting on 3 sts above those bound-off on previous row.
Rib 4 more rows, still inc at corners as before.
Bind off in rib.

## Finishing

Press pieces under a damp cloth. Join seams and press. Sew on buttons.

# Knit one flower one

Gay knitted accessories for a little girl, all trimmed with lazy daisy flowers in brightly colored embroidery.

**Sizes**
**Bolero.** Directions are for 24in chest.
Length to shoulder, 9in.
**Scarf, cap and mittens.**
To fit average 4-year-old.
**Bag.** About 5in square.

> **Gauge**
> 5½ sts and 8 rows to 1in over st st worked on No. 5 needles.
> 15sc and 16 rows to 4in worked on No.I hook

**Materials**
Knitting Worsted
14 ounces
One pair No. 5 needles
(or Canadian No. 8)
Set of 4 No. 5 double-pointed needles
Set of 4 No. 4
(or Canadian No. 9)
double-pointed needles
One No. I (5.50 mm) crochet hook
One No. F (4.00 mm) crochet hook
Tapestry yarn
2 skeins orange
2 skeins white
2 skeins green
2 skeins blue
2 skeins light blue
4 skeins yellow
Red beads, optional
¼ yd. lining material
¼ yd. interlining fabric

**Bolero back**

Using No.5 needles, cast on 65 sts.
Beg with a K row, work 4in st st, ending with a P row.

## Shape armholes

Bind off 3 sts at beg of next 2 rows and 2 sts at beg of next 2 rows.

K2 tog at each end every other row 3 times. 49 sts.

Continue without shaping until armholes measure $4\frac{3}{4}$in from beg, ending with a P row.

## Shape shoulders

Bind off 3 sts at beg of next 8 rows and 2 sts at beg of next 2 rows.

Bind off rem 21 sts.

## Bolero left front

Using No.5 needles, cast on 22 sts.

**1st row** K.

**2nd row** Inc in first st, P to end.

Rep these 2 rows twice more.

**7th row** K.

**8th row** Cast on 2 sts, P to end.

Rep last 2 rows twice more, then rep 1st and 2nd rows twice more. 33 sts.

Continue without shaping until straight edge of work measures same as Back to underarm, ending with a P row.

## Shape armhole

At arm edge, bind off 3 sts. Work 1 row even. Bind off 2 sts at beg of next row.

K2 tog at armhole edge every other row 3 times. 25 sts.

Continue without shaping until armhole measures 2in from beg, ending with a K row.

## Shape neck

At neck edge, bind off 3 sts and 2 sts every other row twice.

K2 tog at neck edge every other row 4 times. 14 sts.

Continue without shaping until armhole measures same as Back to shoulder, ending with a P row.

## Shape shoulder

At arm edge, bind off 3 sts every other row 4 times. P 1 row. Bind off rem 2 sts.

## Bolero right front

Work as given for Left front, reversing all shaping.

## Bag

Using No.5 needles, cast on 27 sts.

Beg with a K row, work 10in st st, ending with a P row. Bind off.

## Cap

Using No.I hook, ch4. Join with ss to first ch to form circle.

▲ *Brightly colored lazy daisy flowers scattered across a bolero and bag*

**1st round** Ch2 to count as first sc, work 5sc into circle. Join with a ss into 2nd of first 2ch. 6 sts.

**2nd round** Ch2, 1sc into same place, 2sc into each sc to end. Join with a ss into 2nd of first 2ch. 12 sts.

**3rd round** Ch2, 2sc into next sc, *1sc into next sc, 2sc into next sc, rep from * to end. Join with a ss into 2nd of first 2ch. 18 sts.

**4th round** Ch2, 1sc into next sc, 2sc into next sc, *1sc into each of next 2sc, 2sc into next sc, rep from * to end. Join with ss to 2nd of first 2ch. 24 sts.

Continue inc 6 sts in this manner on every round until there are 48 sts.

Work 1 round without inc, inc 6 sts in next round. 54 sts.

**\*\*Work 2 rounds without inc, then inc 6 sts in next round. \*\*** 60 sts.

Rep from ** to ** once more. 66 sts.

Work 3 rounds without inc, then inc 6 sts in next round. 72 sts.

Work 6 rounds without shaping.

Change to No.F hook and work 3 rounds more. Fasten off.

## Earflaps

Work as given for Cap until 8th round has been completed. Fasten off.

Make a second earflap in the same manner.

## Scarf

Using No.5 needles, cast on 23 sts.

Beg with a K row, work 22 rows st st.

**Next row** P to end to mark hemline.

Beg with a P row, work 22 rows st st.

**Next row** (WS) P4, *K up 1, P3, rep from * 5 times more, P1. 29 sts.

**Next row** K1, *P1, K1, rep from * to end.

**Next row** P1, *K1, P1, rep from * to end.

Continue in rib for 10in, ending with a WS row.

**Next row** K4, *K2 tog, K2, rep from * 5 times more, K1. 23 sts.

Beg with a P row, work 22 rows st st.

**Next row** K all sts tbl to mark hemline.

Beg with a K row, work 22 rows st st. Bind off.

## Left mitten

Using set of 4 No.4 needles, cast on 34 sts.

Work in rounds of K1, P1, rib for $2\frac{1}{2}$in.

Change to set of 4 No.5 needles.

Work in rounds of st st, every round K, for 12 rounds.

**Divide for thumb**

**Next round** K27, sl next 7 sts onto holder and leave for thumb, cast on 7 sts.

K 15 rounds st st.

**Shape top**

**Next round** K1, sl 1, K1, psso, K11, K2 tog, K2, sl 1, K1, psso, K11, K2 tog, K1.

**Next round** K.

**Next round** K1, sl 1, K1, psso, K9, K2 tog, K2, sl 1, K1, psso, K9, K2 tog, K1.

**Next round** K.

Continue dec in this manner every other round 3 times. 14 sts.

Divide sts onto 2 needles and weave tog.

**Thumb**

**Next round** Sl 7 sts on holder onto No.5 needle, pick up and K 7 sts from cast-on sts at base of thumb. 14 sts.

# Color key charts

**Cap**

**Scarf**

**Bolero**

Divide these sts onto 3 needles and work 11 rounds st st.

**Shape top**
**Next round** K2, *K2 tog, K1, rep from * to end.
**Next round** *K2 tog, rep from * to end.
Break off yarn, thread through rem sts, draw up and fasten off.

## Right mitten

Work as given for Left mitten, reversing position of thumb as follows:
**Next round** Sl first 7 sts onto holder and leave for thumb, cast on 7 sts, K to end.

## Finishing

Press each piece under a damp cloth with a warm iron,

omitting ribbing.
**Bolero**. Join shoulder and side seams. Work embroidery on fronts using darning needle, embroidery yarns and lazy daisy st, working from chart and sewing either red beads or French knots in center of each flower.
**Edging.** Using No.F hook and with RS facing, work 1 row sc around all edges, then work a row of crab st, working in sc from left to right instead of right to left. Press seams.
**Bag.** Cut lining, allowing $\frac{1}{2}$in seam allowances. Cut interlining without seam allowances. Work embroidery as for bolero, working from bag chart. Join side seams.
**Edging.** Work 1 row sc and 1 row crab st around top as given for bolero. Join side

seams of lining. Insert lining and interlining, then slip stitch lining in place around top of bag. Using No.F hook and 3 strands yarn, make a chain about 16in long. Fasten off. Sew one end of chain to each side of top of bag.
**Cap.** Work embroidery on earflaps as given for bolero and working from cap chart. Sew on earflaps.
**Scarf.** Work embroidery on st st sections between hemline and rib at each end as given for bolero, working from the bolero chart.
With RS facing, join sides of hems, turn hems right sides out and slip stitch in place. Press.
**Mittens.** Work embroidery on back of each mitten as for bolero, working from mitten chart.

**Bag**

**Mittens**

1897

# Frilly and feminine

Unashamedly pretty and feminine cushions give the perfect finishing touch to a bedroom. One petalled, the other frilled, both cushions are easy to make and provide a lovely accent.

## Petal cushion

### Size

About 15in diameter.

### Materials

Coats & Clark's O.N.T. Speed-Cro-Sheen
8 (100 yd.) balls
One No. D (3.00 mm) crochet hook
½ yd. lining material 36 in. wide
Pillow form 15 in. diameter

### Front

Using No.D hook, ch8. Join with a ss into first ch to form a ring.

**1st round** Ch6, 1dc into ring, *ch3, 1dc into ring, rep from * 3 times more, ch3, ss to 3rd of 6ch. 6sp.

**2nd round** *Into next loop work 1sc, 1hdc, 3dc, 1hdc, 1sc, rep from * 5 times more.

**3rd round** Ch5, *working into back, make 1sc around stem of next dc of first round, ch5, rep from * 4 times more, join with a ss into first sc.

**4th round** *Into ch5 sp work 1sc, 1hdc, 5dc, 1hdc, 1sc, rep from * to end.

**5th round** *Ch7, 1sc into back of sc between petals of previous round, rep from * 4 times more, ch7, join with a ss into first of first 7ch.

**6th round** *Into ch7 loop work 1sc, 1hdc, 7dc, 1hdc, 1sc, rep from * to end.

**7th round** *Ch9, 1sc into back of sc between petals of previous round, rep from * 4 times more, ch9, join with a ss into first of first 9ch.

**8th round** *Into ch9 loop work 1sc, 1hdc, 9dc, 1hdc, 1sc, rep from * to end.

**9th round** *Ch11, 1 sc into back of sc between petals of previous round, rep from * 4 times more, ch11, join with a ss into first of first 11ch.

**10th round** *Into ch11 loop work 1sc, 1hdc, 11dc, 1hdc, 1sc, rep from * to end.

**11th round** *Ch5, 1 sc between 5th and 6th dc of previous round, ch5, 1sc into back of sc between petals of previous round, rep from * 5 times more, skipping last sc, join with a ss into first of first 5ch. 12 loops.

**12th–19th rounds** As 4th–11th, working the additional number of repeats.

**20th–26th rounds** As 4th–10th, working the additional number of repeats.

**27th and 28th rounds** As 9th and 10th, working additional number of repeats.
Rep last 2 rounds once more.

**31st round** As 9th, working additional repeats.

**32nd round** (picot round) *Into ch11 loop work 1sc, 1hdc, 6dc, ch3, ss into first of 3ch – called 1 picot –, 6dc, 1hdc, 1sc, rep from * to end.

**33rd round** As 9th, working additional repeats.

**34th round** (picot round) *Into ch11 loop work 1sc, 1hdc, 1dc, 5tr, 1 picot, 5tr, 1dc, 1hdc, 1sc, rep from * to end.
Rep last 2 rounds once more. Fasten off.

### Back

Using No.D hook, ch4. Join with a ss into first ch to form a ring.

**1st round** Work 8sc into ring, join with ss to first sc.

**2nd round** Ch4, 1dc into same place as ss, *into next sc ch1, 1dc, ch1, 1dc, rep from * to end, ch1, join with ss to 3rd of 4ch. 16dc.

**3rd round** Ss into first sp, ch4, 1dc into same sp, *into next sp ch1, 1dc, ch1, 1dc, rep from * to end, ch1, join with ss to 3rd of 4ch.

**4th round** Ss into first sp, ch4, *1dc into next sp, ch1, rep from * to end, join with ss to 3rd of 4ch.

**5th round** As 3rd.

**6th–9th rounds** As 4th.

**10th and 11th rounds** Ss into first sp, ch5, *1dc into next sp, ch2, rep from * to end, join with a ss into 3rd of 5ch.

**12th and 13th rounds** Ss into first sp, ch6, *1dc into next sp, ch3, rep from * to end, join with a ss into 3rd of 6ch.

**14th and 15th rounds** Ss into first sp, ch7, *1dc into next sp, ch4, rep from * to end, join with ss to 3rd of 7ch.

**16th round** Into each ch4 sp work 4sc. Fasten off.

## Finishing

Fold lining materials in half and cut a circle 16in diameter. With right sides together, stitch ½in from the edge, leaving an opening of about 10 in. Trim seam and turn right sides out. Insert pillow form and hand stitch opening.
With right sides together, hand stitch the crocheted cover Back to Front, leaving an opening of about 10in. Turn right sides out, insert pillow and stitch opening.

## Frilled pillow

### Size

About 15in diameter.

### Materials

Coats & Clark's O.N.T. Speed-Cro-Sheen
9 (100 yd.) balls
One No. D (3.00 mm) crochet hook
½ yd. lining material 36 in. wide
Pillow form 15 in. diameter

### Front

Using No.D hook, ch4. Join with ss to form a ring.

**1st round** Work 8sc into ring, join with ss to first sc.

**2nd round** *Ch6, 1sc into next sc, rep from * 6 times more, ch3, 1dc into last sc. 8 loops.

**3rd round** *Ch3, 1sc into

*Detail showing the surface crochet technique using a contrast color on the second row of the frill*

▲ *Two delicate crochet pillows in white make a pretty centerpiece for a very feminine bedroom*

next ch6 loop, rep from * to end, 1sc into dc.

**4th round** *Ch6, 1sc into next sc, ch6, 1sc into next ch3 loop, ch6, 1sc into next sc, rep from * until two ch3 loops rem, ch6, 1sc into next sc, ch6, 1sc into next ch3 loop, ch3, 1dc into first of first 6ch.

Rep 3rd and 4th rounds 4 times more, then 3rd round once.

**14th round** *Ch6, 1sc into next sc, rep from * to end, ch3, 1dc into first of first 6ch.

Rep 3rd and 14th rounds 3 times more, then 3rd round once. Fasten off.

**Frills**

Starting at center and working outward, attach yarn to any ch6 loop on the 2nd round, *work 6sc into ch6 loop taking yarn around ch and not into it, rep from * to end of round. Join with ss to first sc. Fasten off.

Attach yarn to any ch6 loop on 4th round and work 8sc into each ch6 loop as before.

Work as for 4th round on 6th and every other round.

Attach yarn to first frill and work 1sc into each sc. Join with ss to first sc and fasten off.

Work a second layer to each frill in the same manner.

**Back**

Work as given for Back of Petal pillow.

**Finishing**

Finish as given for Petal pillow but join Back and Front of crocheted cover by placing wrong sides together and working sc through the double thickness.

# For special occasions

Here is a charming party dress to make for a little girl. The dress has been made up in a printed velveteen with an eyelet embroidery yoke, but the pattern looks equally pretty made in summery fabrics.

## Requirements

### Yardages
**Main fabric,** 36-inch width, with nap: ages 5 and 6, 1½ yards; age 7, 1¾ yards; age 8, 2 yards.
**Contrast fabric,** 36-inch width: ⅜ yard for all sizes.

### Notions
☐ 1-in square graph paper for pattern
☐ one 12-inch zipper
☐ two small snap fasteners
☐ 1½ yards ½-inch wide lace trim

## Pattern and cutting out

### Pattern sizing
Back neck to hem lengths: age 5, 20 inches; age 6, 22 inches; age 7, 24 inches; age 8, 26 inches.
Draw the pattern to scale on graph paper and transfer any markings given on the graph.
Add following seam and hem allowances to the pattern: ¾ inch center back, 2 inches hem and ½ inch all other edges.

### Cutting out
Following the appropriate layout for the size you are making (figure 1a, b), cut out back, front and sleeve pieces from main fabric. Note the pile direction if you are using velveteen.
Cut also two sleevebands (**a**) 4 inches deep and to these lengths: for age 5, 9 inches; age 6, 9½ inches; age 7, 10 inches; age 8, 10½ inches. Following figure 2, cut out yoke in contrast fabric.
Cut also two neckband pieces (**b**) 2 inches deep to these lengths: for age 5, 12¾ inches; age 6, 13¼ inches; age 7, 13¾ inches; age 8, 14¼ inches.

## Making the dress

Work two rows of machine gatherings on the seamline of the crown of the sleeve between balance marks from 'A' to 'B' and then between the balance marks at the yoke edge of the front piece. Work gathering stitches along lower edge of the sleeves 1 inch in from the sides.
Stitch the center back seam, right sides together, leaving 12¾ inches open from top edge for the zipper. Press seam open. Insert zipper, starting ⅝ inch down from the neck edge.
Cut a 30-inch length of lace and work machine gathering ⅛ inch from the raw edge.
With right sides together and finished edge of trim inward, stitch trim to contrast yoke ⅜ inch from edge, placing extra gathers at the curves (figure 3).
With right sides together, pin center front of contrast yoke to center front of front piece at point 'C'. Draw up the gathers of the front piece to fit the yoke and stitch. Press seam toward yoke and overcast to make neat.
Stitch shoulder, side and sleeve seams. Press seams open and make neat.
With right sides together, stitch narrow ends of sleeveband to form a circle. Press seam open.
Draw up gathers at the lower edge of sleeves to fit sleevebands. Place one long raw edge of sleeveband to sleeve edge, right sides together, and stitch. Make opposite raw edge neat.
Press seam allowance toward band. Following figure 4, turn neat edge to inside of sleeve to make the finished width of band 1½ inches. Topstitch in place through first seamline.
Pin sleeve into armhole, matching balance mark on top of crown to shoulder seam.
Draw up the gathered sleeve crown to fit armhole and stitch. Make a second row of stitching in the seam allowance ¼ inch from first line. Trim to 1/16 inch from second row. Make neat.
Cut 24-inch length of lace for neck. Gather to fit one long edge of one neckband piece, folding under raw ends of trim to make neat. Finish as for yoke trim.
Place neckband pieces together, right sides facing. Stitch along short ends and trimmed edge. Turn to right side. Turn in seam allowance along facing edge of double neckband and stitch (figure 5).
With right sides together, stitch raw edge of neckband to neck edge of dress. Topstitch along the neck seamline through all layers to catch the neckband facing in place.
Sew two snap fasteners at back of neckband. Turn up hem and hand fell.

BACK  FRONT

▼ **1a.** *Layout for 36 inch fabric, sizes 5, 6 and 7*

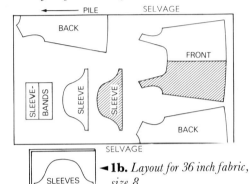

◀ **1b.** *Layout for 36 inch fabric, size 8*

**2.** *Layout for 36 inch contrast fabric, all sizes* ▼

KEY
Age 5 length 20in
Age 6 length 22in
Age 7 length 24in
Age 8 length 26in

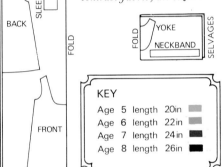

**3.** *Positioning the lace trim on the contrast yoke*

**4.** *Finished sleeveband*

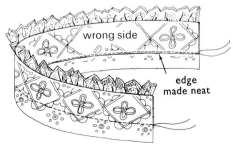

**5.** *Trimmed neckband showing lower edge made neat*

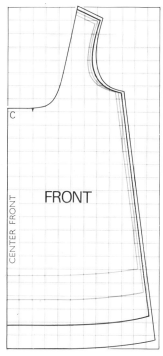

FRONT

CENTER FRONT

C

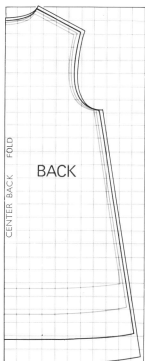

BACK

CENTER BACK FOLD

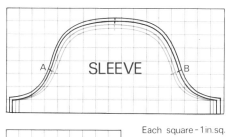

SLEEVE

A          B

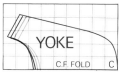

YOKE

C.F. FOLD          C

Each square - 1 in. sq.

Add ¾ inch seam allowance on center back, 2 inches hem allowance and ½ inch seam on all other edges.

# Motifs
# to have
# fun with

The fun and challenge of embroidery or needlepoint lies in the embroiderer's own ability to adapt an idea for the piece of work at hand. The result might be a tiny needlepoint change purse with a single figure on it, or a colorful appliqué quilt with a scattering of motifs. The scope of possibilities is limited only by one's imagination.

Here are some delightful motifs suitable for working either singly or in groups. Small fashion accessories such as belts and buckles, purses and wallets could be made in needlepoint using a single motif and make perfect gifts. Pillows could be worked with the same motif repeated as an all-over pattern, or with one motif enlarged. Repeat one motif, or combine

several, on a needlepoint bellpull or for a tote bag shoulder strap. One small figure worked in cross-stitch near the neckline of a tee-shirt would add an interesting personal touch, and an old, battered pair of jeans can be given a new look with a cross-stitched figure worked on one pocket, or perhaps at the knee.

The choice of threads and fabrics would determine the impact of even a single figure in embroidery: worked in crewel wool on a bright, sturdy fabric, the finished piece has a rather informal air. If embroidery floss is used on a fine background such as silk the motif is transformed into a more formal means of decoration.

1903

1904

# Pink, white, blue - and pretty

You'll find this pretty bat-wing sweater with its big, full sleeves very easy to make — it only requires the simplest of shaping. The sweater was designed by Patricia Roberts, who chose the pastel sugared-almond shades of pink, blue and white. The fluffy mohair wool she used is a perfect complement to the soft lines of the garment.

## Sizes

Directions are for 32in bust. The figures in brackets [ ] refer to the 34 and 36in sizes respectively.
Length from cuff to cuff, 53½[54½ : 55½]in.
Length to shoulder, 18[18½ : 18¾]in.

## Gauge

8 sts and 10 rows to 1 in over st st worked on No.4 needles.

## Materials

Bucilla Melody
16 [17:18] 1 oz. balls main color A, white
Bucilla Fingering Yarn
2 1 oz. balls color B, blue
2 1 oz. balls color C, pink
One pair No. 3 needles (or Canadian No. 10)
One pair No. 4 needles (or Canadian No. 9)

## Right side

Using No.3 needles and A, beg at sleeve edge and cast on 64[68:68] sts.
Work even for 24 rows in K2, P2 rib.
Continue in rib, inc one st at each end of next and every following 8th row, eight times in all. 80[84:84] sts.
Work even for 7 rows.
**Next row** Inc 1[K2:inc 1], *pick up the loop between the needles, slip it onto the left-hand needle and K tbl – called pick up 1 –, K1, rep from * ending last rep, pick up 1, K1[3:1]. 160[164:168] sts.
Change to No.4 needles.
Work 3 rows st st, beg with a P row.
Continue in st st, working patt as follows and attaching and breaking off contrast colors as required.
**1st row** K2[4:2] sts C, *4 sts A, 4 sts C, rep from * ending last rep 2[4:2] sts C.
**2nd row** P2[4:2] sts C, *4 sts A, 4 sts C, rep from * ending last rep 2[4:2] sts C.
**3rd row** As 1st.
**4th row** P2[4:2] sts A, *4 sts C, 4 sts A, rep from * ending last rep 2[4:2] sts A.
**5th row** K2[4:2] sts A, *4 sts C, 4 sts A, rep from * ending last rep 2[4:2] sts A.
**6th row** As 4th.

**7th–9th rows** As 1st–3rd.
**10th and 11th rows** Work in A only.
**12th and 13th rows** Work in C only.
**14th and 15th rows** Work in A only.
**16th row** P4[6:4] sts A, *using B P1, turn, K twice into this st, turn, P these 2 sts tog tbl – called bobble 1 –, P7 sts A, rep from * ending last rep 3[5:3] sts A.
**17th–19th rows** Work in A only.
**20th row** P8[2:8] sts A, *using B bobble 1, P7 sts A, rep from * ending last rep 7[1:7] sts A.
**21st–23rd rows** Work in A only.
**24th–27th rows** As 16th–19th.
**28th and 29th rows** Work in B only.
**30th–32nd rows** Work in A only.
These 32 rows form patt. Rep them twice more, then work first 10 rows once, marking each end of the last row with a colored thread.
Continue in patt for 46[50:54] rows more.**

### Divide for neck

**Next row** Work across 74[78:82] sts. Slip these sts on a holder, bind off 10 sts, work across rem 76 sts.
Continue on these sts.

### Back

Continue in patt for 29 rows more. Bind off.

### Front

Attach yarn at inner edge of sts on holder.
Continuing in patt, dec one st at neck on each of next 72[76:80] rows. Fasten off rem 2 sts as if they were one.

## Left side

Work as given for RS, working only 45[49:54] rows at ** before dividing for neck.

## Back ribbing

Join center back seam.
Using No.3 needles and A, with RS facing, pick up and K114[120:128] sts between marker threads.

Work 88 rows K2, P2 rib.
Bind off loosely in rib.

## Front ribbing

Using No.3 needles and A, with RS facing, pick up and K112[120:128] sts from right front after marker thread.
Work 88 rows K2, P2 rib.
Bind off loosely in rib.

## Neck edging

Using No.3 needles and B, cast on 6 sts.
**1st row** Inc 1, K3, dec 1.
**2nd** row P.
Rep these 2 rows until edging measures same as neck edge of sweater. Sew in place, binding off only when correct length is obtained.

## Collar

Using No.4 needles and A, cast on 122 sts.
Work 8 rows K2, P2 rib, beg RS rows with K2 and WS rows with P2.
Continue in rib and keeping edges as established, inc one st at each end of next and following 10th rows 4 times in all. 130 sts.
Continue without shaping for 9 rows more. Bind off loosely in rib.

## Edging

Using No.3 needles and B, with RS facing, pick up and K40 sts from straight edge of collar, 130 sts from bound-off edge and 40 sts from other straight edge. 210 sts.
**1st row** Inc purlwise in every st. 420 sts.
**Next row** K.
Using No.4 needle, bind off knitwise.

## Finishing

Press all st st pieces on WS under a damp cloth with a warm iron.
Slip stitch lower edge of left front in position behind right front.
Press seams.
Join sleeve and side seams.
Sew cast-on edge of collar in place on WS at base of edging so that it rolls over the edging to RS.

# NEEDLEPOINT FOLIO

## Stitch a stool top

This needlepoint stool top would add a note of color and interest to any room. The work is an abstract composition of stitches – similar to a sampler – in which color and shade play equal parts in the impact of the whole design.

### Ideas for using the design

Worked on a finer mesh canvas, the completed piece would be proportionately smaller – 9¾ inches square using canvas with 16 single threads to the inch, for instance – for a box top, a purse or a small decorative panel. Using chunky knitting yarn on rug canvas, the design becomes an attractive rug. Or use the materials listed below but make the design as a pillow, picking up one of the colors in the work for the edging.

### Materials required for the stool top

The area to be worked for the stool top illustrated is 11¾ inches square, with adjoining side panels 1¾ inches deep. Materials given are for the green and purple color scheme, although a green and gold variation is shown as one effective alternative.

☐ ⅝ yard 26 inch single thread canvas (14 threads to the inch)
☐ No.20 tapestry needle
☐ D.M.C. Tapestry yarn in the follow-

9 skeins 7379 dark olive green; 4 skeins each 7364 medium olive green, 7361 light olive green; 1 skein each 7245 dark purple, 7257 purple, 7253 pale lilac, 7306 dark hyacinth, 7241 light hyacinth, 7157 dark fuchsia, 7155 light fuchsia

☐ D.M.C. 6-strand floss in the following colors and quantities:
3 skeins 552 dark violet; 2 skeins each 553 medium violet, 554 light violet, 3346 moss green; 1 skein each 3685 dark cyclamen, 3687 medium cyclamen

☐ Upholstered stool, without cover

## To work the design

The stitches used in making the stool top are indicated on the working chart. The background area which is incorporated in the design is worked in lines of satin stitch in varying widths. Two shades of green yarn are merged at random. All stitches in these areas are worked in the same direction except those in two of the side panels, so that these are consistent in direction when the stool has been completed.

## Blocking the canvas

If the needlepoint has not been done on a frame, it should be blocked to restore the canvas to its original shape. Most stitches distort the canvas because of their diagonal pull. Needlepoint should never be pressed with an iron, as this flattens the textured stitches and ruins the appearance of the work.

Dampen the back of the work with cold water. Cover a flat surface with several sheets of white blotting paper. Place the work face down on the board and pin out at one-inch intervals, using rust-proof thumbtacks. Pull the work gently into shape, adjusting the thumbtacks. Dampen the work again thoroughly and leave for at least 24 hours, away from heat. When the work is completely dry, check for any missed stitches and fill them in at this stage.

Cover the stool.

▼ *The abstract design makes a handsome stool top*

▲ *Detail reveals a variety of stitches and threads    Alternative colors* ▼

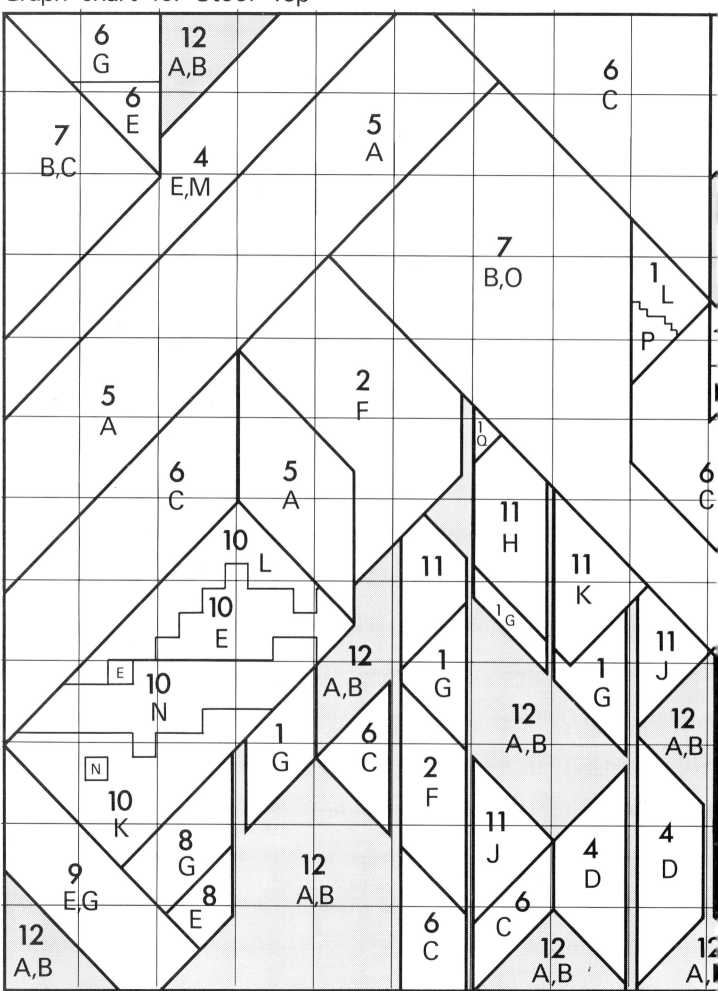

# Stitch and color key

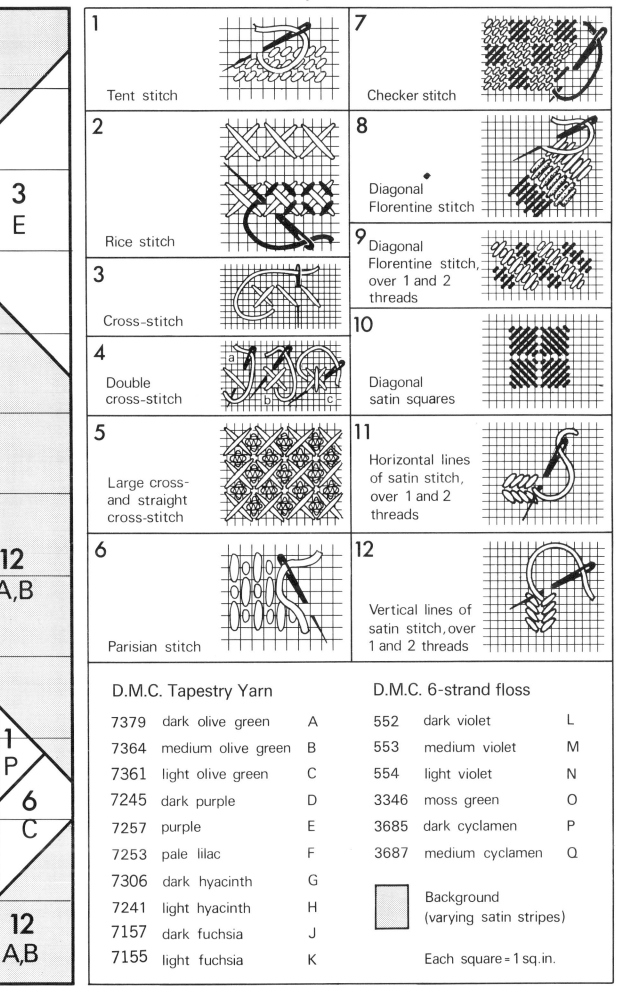

| | | | |
|---|---|---|---|
| **1** Tent stitch | | **7** Checker stitch | |
| **2** Rice stitch | | **8** Diagonal Florentine stitch | |
| **3** Cross-stitch | | **9** Diagonal Florentine stitch, over 1 and 2 threads | |
| **4** Double cross-stitch | | **10** Diagonal satin squares | |
| **5** Large cross- and straight cross-stitch | | **11** Horizontal lines of satin stitch, over 1 and 2 threads | |
| **6** Parisian stitch | | **12** Vertical lines of satin stitch, over 1 and 2 threads | |

## D.M.C. Tapestry Yarn

| | | |
|---|---|---|
| 7379 | dark olive green | A |
| 7364 | medium olive green | B |
| 7361 | light olive green | C |
| 7245 | dark purple | D |
| 7257 | purple | E |
| 7253 | pale lilac | F |
| 7306 | dark hyacinth | G |
| 7241 | light hyacinth | H |
| 7157 | dark fuchsia | J |
| 7155 | light fuchsia | K |

## D.M.C. 6-strand floss

| | | |
|---|---|---|
| 552 | dark violet | L |
| 553 | medium violet | M |
| 554 | light violet | N |
| 3346 | moss green | O |
| 3685 | dark cyclamen | P |
| 3687 | medium cyclamen | Q |

Background (varying satin stripes)

Each square = 1 sq. in.

# Dyes from nature

Although natural dyeing takes longer than synthetic dyeing, the colors obtained are often more attractive than those produced by modern chemical dyes. Natural dyes produce a certain luster and softness in the fabric or yarn they are applied to that chemicals do not give, and it is rewarding, too, to select plants or berries from the garden or field and use them to produce a beautifully colored yarn or fabric.

Most plants will produce staining juices if crushed and boiled, but comparatively few produce a fast dye when applied to fabric or yarn. Some of these plants produce staining juices which are known as "adjective" or "mordant" dyes: that is the fabric or yarn to be dyed must be subjected to a preparatory bath containing a metallic mineral, or mordant, to enable the dye to penetrate the yarn fibers. There are also a few substantive, or non-mordant dyes that do not require a fixing agent. These include the lichens and walnuts. In most cases, however, mordanting is a vital process, for an unevenly mordanted yarn or fabric will not dye evenly.

Wool is easy to mordant, as the fibers are porous, but silk, cotton and linen are more difficult; silk has to be steeped for a long time in a tepid or cold mordant, and often loses its luster, and cotton and linen fibers are so tough that it is difficult to get the mordant to penetrate evenly. For the beginner, then, wool is the best fiber to dye.

Wool to be dyed must be put through the following processes: scouring (washing, to remove any dust or grease), mordanting and dyeing.

Different mordants can produce a darker or brighter dye effect, besides preparing the fabric for the dye.

## Mordants

There are many mordants, but the three most commonly used are the following:

### Potassium aluminum sulphate (alum)
This is the most commonly used mordant. Use 4 oz, dissolved in a little cold water with 1 oz cream of tartar, per lb of thick wool, and 3 oz with 1 oz cream of tartar, for thin wool. This produces clear colors.

### Bichromate of potash (chrome)
This mordant gives wool a soft and silky feel, mellowing the shade. Use $\frac{1}{2}$ oz chrome with 1 oz cream of tartar to 1 lb of wool. A lid should be placed on the mordant bath, as chrome is very sensitive to light. The wool should not be exposed to light after mordanting. It should be rinsed and, if it is not to be dyed immediately, shut in a drawer or put in a linen bag.

### Stannous chloride (tin)
Tin can be used as a mordant, or it can be added to a dyebath toward the end of dyeing to brighten the color. It should always be carefully dissolved before adding to a dyebath made of galvanized iron, as it destroys the surface of the vessel. Used as a mordant, the ratio is $\frac{1}{2}$ oz tin and 2 oz cream of tartar to 1 lb of wool, used as for alum. The cream of tartar should be dissolved in water before adding the tin. To brighten a shade, a few tin crystals should be added to an alum mordant.

## Dyeing equipment

### You will need
- ☐ 1 lb of the natural dye of your choice per 1 lb dry weight of yarn or fabric
- ☐ 2 galvanized iron, enamel or stainless steel buckets (one for dye, one for mordanting)
- ☐ 1 package soap flakes (*not* chemical detergent)
- ☐ Kitchen scales
- ☐ Water thermometer
- ☐ Smooth wood sticks to handle yarn or fabric during dyeing
- ☐ The mordant of your choice
- ☐ Cream of tartar

## The mordanting process

### Preparation
Wool must be thoroughly washed, or scoured, before being mordanted and

*These colors were obtained from a range of common plants including walnut skins, privet leaves, gorse flowers, marsh marigold flowers, dog's mercury, blackberry shoots, onion skins, bracken fern, lichens and oak bark* ▼

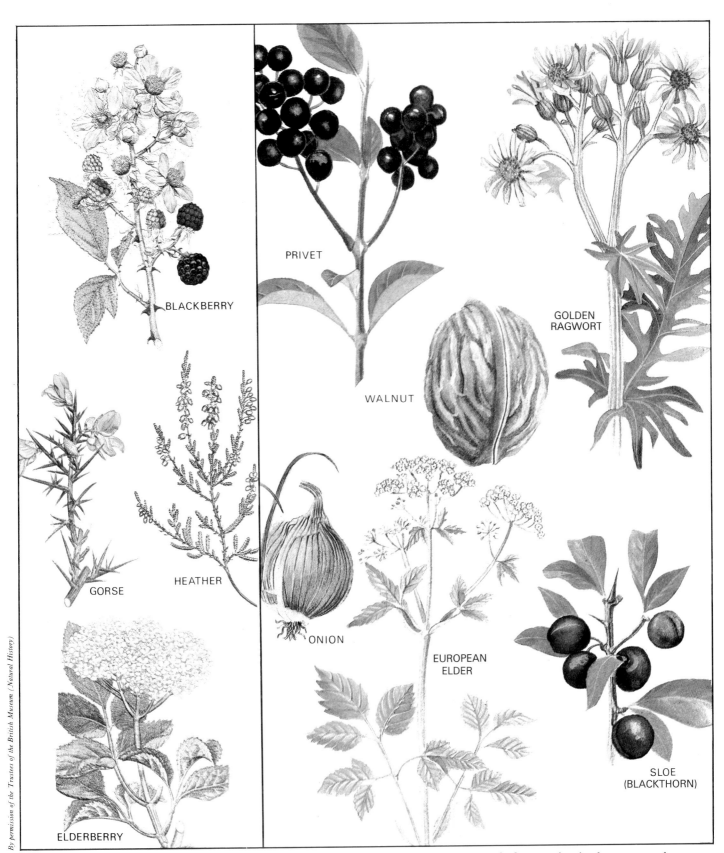

BLACKBERRY

PRIVET

GOLDEN
RAGWORT

WALNUT

GORSE

HEATHER

ONION

EUROPEAN
ELDER

SLOE
(BLACKTHORN)

ELDERBERRY

dyed, to remove all fat and dirt. If this is not done the color cannot be fast as the dirt and grease absorb the dye. Steep the wool in hot water until thoroughly soaked, then allow to cool. Work up a warm soap lather in a bucket, immerse the wool and work it very gently. Rinse in water of the same temperature, then repeat the process, treating the wool gently at all times. Squeeze, but do not twist. The wool can be mordanted while still damp.

Skeins of yarn should be tied in a loose figure-eight tie, so the mordant can penetrate to all parts easily. Be careful that they are not too tightly tied, or the mordant will not soak in and the result will be white patches on the wool after dyeing.

Make sure the mordant is quite dissolved before putting in the yarn, or there may be bad stains on the finished article. Always see that the saucepan or bucket is quite big enough for the yarn and do not stir too vigorously or the wool will become "felted".

**The process**

Dissolve the appropriate amount of mordant and cream of tartar in a little

1911

cold water and add to a large bucket of cool water. Stir well, and heat. Remember that chrome mordant must be covered, as it is sensitive to light. As the water warms, add the wool, which should be wetted beforehand, and bring slowly to boiling point. Then let it simmer: one hour for thick yarn or fabric, three-quarters of an hour for finer qualities. Lift out the wool with a smooth wood stick and let it drain for a moment. Squeeze excess moisture from it but do not wring or wash it. The wool can be dyed immediately, but is better left in a linen bag overnight, or longer.

## Dyes

The usual quantity necessary to produce a medium shade of a natural dye is 1 lb of dye-plant to 1 lb dry weight of yarn or fabric.

### To prepare a dye
Most dye-plants need to be crushed (berries) or chopped (leaves, flowers or stems), added to a bucket of cold water and then heated. When boiling point is reached, the dye is simmered for a time. Most dyes are then allowed to cool and left to stand overnight.

### Dyeing wool
Having chosen and prepared the dye of your choice, follow the instructions given for that dye. After the wool is lifted from the bath, the excess dye should be gently squeezed from it, and the wool rinsed until the water runs clear. A hot soapy wash will then improve and set the color, after which the yarn or fabric should be dried.

## Plants used in dyeing

### Birch bark
Birch bark should be chopped up small, added to cold water, heated, then when boiling point is reached, simmered for two to three hours. Leave to cool, let it stand overnight, then add the fabric or yarn to be dyed, bring back to the boil and simmer until the required depth of color is reached. Birch bark produces plum color, which becomes brown with the addition of iron mordant and a dull, deep gold with alum.

### Blackberries
The young shoots of blackberries, picked in spring, should be boiled with the yarn for an hour or more, iron mordant and cream of tartar added (see mordant chart for amounts) and dyeing continued for half an hour to yield a deep, almost black color. The berries, which produce a bluish-gray color, should be

crushed, put in cold water and brought to the boil. The yarn, which should be mordanted with alum before immersion, is placed in the dye and simmered until the required depth of color is obtained.

### Bracken fern shoots
Pick the shoots in spring while they are still curled, put in cold water, bring gradually to the boil and simmer for two hours, then cool. Use alum mordant on the yarn to be dyed; place this, after mordanting, in the dye, and simmer again for two hours. This produces a clear, yellowish-green color.

### Dog's mercury
The whole plant can be used. Should be gathered in early spring and chopped before being added to cold water in the dyebath and brought to the boil. Use 2 lb of the plant to 1 lb of wool. Alum mordant should be used on the yarn to be dyed. Immerse the mordanted yarn when dye is boiling and simmer until the desired color, is reached. Produces a yellow-green color.

### Elder
The leaves give a green color, treated as for birch bark and used on alum mordanted yarn. The berries give a lilac-blue color with alum mordanted yarn with 1 oz salt added to the mordant, and a violet color with alum mordant alone. Prepare as for privet berries.

### Gorse flowers
Gorse flowers can be used alone or with young shoots. Boil the flowers or young shoots for one hour, strain, and add to a dyebath half-full of cold water. Use 1 lb. of the plant to 1 lb. of yarn. Repeat the process and add yarn that has been mordanted with alum, simmering until the desired color is reached. Produces a strong yellow.

### Heather shoots
Ling is the best type of heather to use. Bring it gradually to the boil, simmer for three to four hours, cool and stand overnight. Alum mordant should be used on the yarn to be dyed (4 oz alum and 2 oz cream of tartar to 1 lb of yarn), which should then be added to the dyebath. Bring this back to the boil, and simmer for one hour. Produces olive yellow.

### Lichens (non-mordant)
Lichens should be scraped off walls or rocks, well bruised and crumbled, if dry. Put alternate layers of lichen and yarn into the dyebath. Fill the dyebath with cool water and bring slowly to the boil. Simmer for some hours until the required

depth of color is reached. Wash well. The color will be very fast and range from dark auburn brown to pinky orange or pale yellow.

### Onion skins
Use only the outer skins. Boil for about two hours and then immerse the yarn, which should have been mordanted with alum. This produces golden brown. Tin added toward the end of dyeing produces orange brown. Hang the yarn in the open air to remove the smell. Not a very durable dye.

### Privet berries
Crush the berries before adding them to a dyebath of cold water ($1\frac{1}{2}$ lb berries to 1 lb yarn) and use alum mordant on the yarn to be dyed. Dye as for birch bark. Produces a bluish green.

### Privet leaves
Soak leaves overnight in cold water. Bring gradually to the boil and simmer for thirty minutes. Strain and cool. Proceed as for birch bark, with alum mordanted yarn. Produces a yellow color.

### Golden ragwort
Chop flower heads into small pieces. Put into a bucket of cold water; bring gradually to the boil and simmer for two to three hours. Allow to grow cold. Next day, heat again, to just below boiling point, immerse alum mordanted yarn and simmer until required depth of color is reached.

### Sloe berries
Treat as for privet berries. Produces slate blue.

### Walnuts (non-mordant)
Collect when ripe, put in a cask and cover with water. Leave for several weeks and use the liquid as a dye, when required. No mordant is necessary. A brown color is obtained; the longer the walnuts are left in the cask, the darker the color. The husks can be boiled for half an hour and allowed to cool. The yarn is then immersed and the dye is boiled until the desired shade is reached.

### Weld (wild mignonette)
The plants should be gathered before seeding. The whole plant except the root is dried and chopped up small, placed in a bucket of cold water, simmered for several hours and cooled, before dyeing proceeds. Weld on an alum mordanted yarn gives lemon yellow and on chrome gives golden yellow. With tin it gives yellow orange and, with iron, olive yellow.

# Circular tablecloths

Round tables, space saving and fashionable, look attractive in any setting. Here are full instructions for making two kinds of elegant circular cloths.

A circular tablecloth can be made in one of two ways.

In the first method (A) which is more suitable for patterned fabric, the round cloth is produced from a square of fabric, each side of the square being the same length as the required diameter of the finished cloth.

It is possible to buy fabrics suitable for tablecloths in wider than usual widths. In most cases, though, the fabric has to be joined at the sides to produce the full width of the square from which the cloth is to be cut.

The second method of making a circular tablecloth (B) involves cutting a circular piece of cloth to fit the table top, plus seam allowance, and joining two curved pieces to it, for the overhang.

This method uses more fabric, but is more suitable than the first for plain fabrics, as method A produces a cloth with side seams which would show in a plain cloth.

### Choosing fabrics
Washable dress or home furnishing fabrics, such as cotton, linen, lawn, man-made fiber mixtures and cotton lace are all suitable for tablecloths. Sheets, available in a variety of patterns and colors, are also suitable, because of their quality and width. For a nursery or kitchen table, vinyl is a good choice, although it does not hang as well as cotton fabric.

### Deciding the size of a circular table-cloth
The cloth should cover the table and should have a generous overhang all around, ranging from about 10 inches to floor level. The actual measurement depends upon personal choice.

▲ **1.** *Measuring for the overhang*

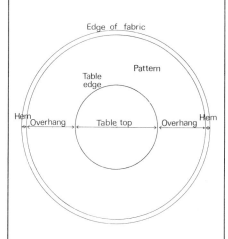

▲ **2.** *Taking measurements for cloth pattern*

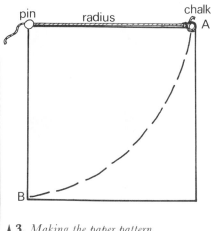

▲ **3.** *Making the paper pattern*

### To determine the depth of the over-hang
Lay a tape measure across the table top and let one end drop down until it reaches the required depth for the overhang (figure 1).

### To find the diameter of the cloth
Measure the diameter of the table top, add this measurement to twice the depth of the overhang, and add $\frac{1}{2}$ inch all around, for hem (figure 2).

### Making a cloth by method A
If the width of the fabric chosen is less than the diameter of the tablecloth, more fabric will have to be joined to the sides of the main piece, so that the width and the length of the fabric, when the pieces are joined, are each equal to the diameter of the cloth.

## Making the tablecloth pattern for method A

### You will need:
- [ ] A large square of paper, with each side a little longer than the radius (half the diameter) of the proposed tablecloth
- [ ] A piece of string 6 inches longer than the radius of the cloth
- [ ] A stick of chalk
- [ ] Several thumbtacks

### To draw the pattern
Work on a flat surface that will not be spoiled if pins are pushed into it.

Tie one end of the string around the chalk. Starting at the chalk end, measure out the radius of the cloth, including $\frac{1}{2}$ inch hem allowance, along the length of the string. Mark this measurement by pushing a thumbtack through the string at this point. Pin the brown paper down on the flat working surface and push the thumbtack, retaining the string on the point of the pin, into the top left-hand corner of the paper.

Hold the thumbtack firmly with one hand and draw an arc with the chalk from A, at the top right-hand corner of the paper, to B, at the bottom left-hand corner (figure 3).

The pattern thus produced is a quarter of the area of the cloth, plus $\frac{1}{2}$ inch hem allowance.

## Making a round cloth, method A

### You will need:
- [ ] Fabric for the cloth
- [ ] Trimming, if required, of your own choice (amount required is four times the length of the arc A to B shown in figure 3, plus 1 inch for overlap). Fringe, braid or guipure lace daisy edging are all suitable
- [ ] Suitable matching thread
- [ ] Matching bias binding (the same amount as for the trimming)
- [ ] Pins
- [ ] Basting thread

*A short cloth is pretty and informal, while the floor-length one adds a touch of elegance*

## Preparing the fabric

If the fabric has to be joined, add pieces to the sides of the main fabric piece; a seam across the middle of the cloth would be very noticeable and could upset the balance of dishes when the table is laid.

Figures 4 and 5 show how to cut and join 48 inch widths to make a round cloth with a diameter of 6 feet 5 inches (77 inches) and a $\frac{1}{2}$ inch hem. Remember that seam allowances for the joins have to be added.

Join the widths with a flat fell seam, stitched with right sides facing (figure 6). You should now have a square of fabric with each side equal to the diameter of the cloth, plus hem allowance.

## Cutting out

Fold the prepared square of fabric in half, then in half again, and pin the pattern onto the folded fabric, as shown in figure 7. Cut along the curved pattern edge. Unpin the pattern and unfold the fabric. Snip V-shaped notches into the edge of the cloth, $\frac{3}{8}$ inch deep, at 1 inch intervals (figure 8). Turn the edge in $\frac{1}{2}$ inch to the wrong side, pin and baste it down. The notches will close up, allowing the hem to curve (figure 9).

## Binding the hem

Pin and baste the bias binding over the turned hem, to cover the raw edge. Stitch on the bias binding (figure 10), turning under the raw ends to make neat.

# Making a round cloth, method B

This method involves cutting a circular piece of fabric the same size as the table top, plus $\frac{1}{2}$ inch seam allowance all around, and adding two curved overhang pieces. Thus the fabric to be used should be of a width equal to the diameter of the table top, plus $\frac{1}{2}$ inch seam allowance all around, and be long enough to cut the overlap pieces.

## Measuring for the pattern

Double the overhang of the cloth and add to it the diameter of the table top, plus 1 inch for seam allowance.

## To make the pattern

Make a paper pattern of a quarter of the area of the cloth, as for method A, then draw a smaller arc within the larger arc, the radius the same as the table-top radius, plus $\frac{1}{2}$ inch for turnings. Cut along this shorter line, reserving the outer piece of pattern, for the overhang.

## To cut out the cloth

Cut off a square of fabric from the main

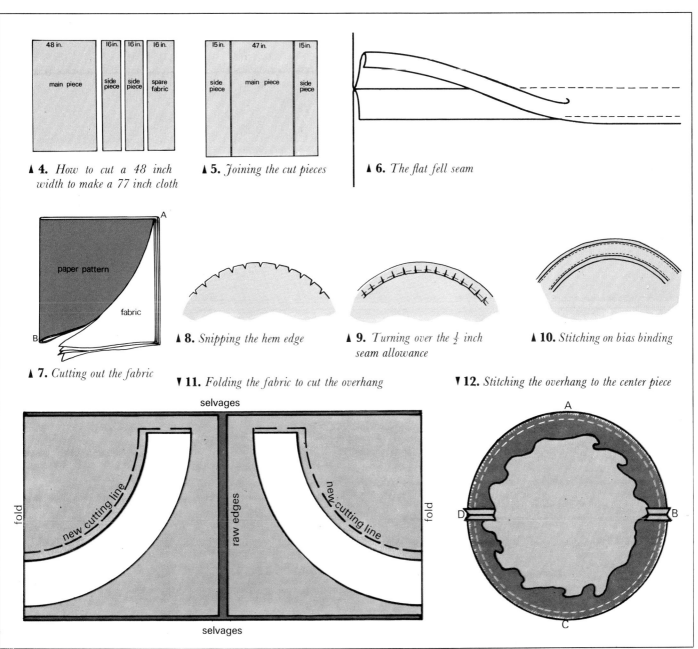

▲ 4. *How to cut a 48 inch width to make a 77 inch cloth*

▲ 5. *Joining the cut pieces*

▲ 6. *The flat fell seam*

▲ 7. *Cutting out the fabric*

▲ 8. *Snipping the hem edge*

▲ 9. *Turning over the ½ inch seam allowance*

▲ 10. *Stitching on bias binding*

▼ 11. *Folding the fabric to cut the overhang*

▼ 12. *Stitching the overhang to the center piece*

length with each side equal to the diameter of the table top, plus ½ inch seam allowance all around. Fold this square in half and in half again, as for method A, and pin the table-top pattern piece to the folded fabric, again as for method A. Cut out around the curve.

Before unfolding the fabric, mark the straight grain four times at four opposite points on the cloth, by making several basting stitches in from the edge, along the folds. These stitches will act as guide lines when attaching the overhang, insuring the grain runs straight on the pieces, so the cloth hangs correctly.

Lay the remaining length of fabric flat on the floor and fold over the ends, so they meet in the center (figure 11).

Pin the pattern piece for the overhang on the fabric, so that one straight edge is on one of the folds. Using chalk, mark on the fabric the cutting line for the inner edge of the overhang, 1 inch from the

inner curve of the pattern.

Mark another line ½ inch from the straight edge of the pattern which is not on the fold of the fabric (figure 11). Cut along the chalked lines and along the outer edge of the pattern, but do not cut along the fold.

Unpin the pattern and pin the pattern to the fabric at the other fold. Mark the cutting lines as for the first piece. Cut out in the same way.

Clip ⅜ inch into the inner edge of both overhang pieces, at 1 inch intervals. With right sides facing, and overhang on top, match the center of the inner edge of one overhanging piece to one of the basting marks on the table-top piece (figure 12). Working outward from this point, pin the overhang to the table-top piece, ½ inch in from the edge. The clips will open out.

Pin the other overhang piece to the table-top piece in a similar way, match-

ing the center to opposite basting mark. Where the overhang pieces meet, pin the raw edges together, adjusting the short seamlines so the overhang fits the table top exactly. Baste and machine stitch these seams. Press them open and make the raw edges neat.

Baste and machine stitch the overhang to the table top. Remove the basting and press the seam allowance down onto the overhang, all around. Overcast the raw edges together. Stitch on the bias binding around the hem, as for the tablecloth made by method A.

## Trimming

Trim around tablecloths with ball fringe, or guipure lace daisy edging. To trim a cloth made by method B, piping in a contrasting color could be added to the seam joining the overhang to the center piece.

# YOUNG IDEA
## Pretty boxes to make

▲ *Some original and funny ideas for boxes to make and decorate yourself*

Making boxes to store things in is easy; look around the house and see how many household objects would make good containers.

Lump sugar boxes can be covered in colored paper or felt and used to store beads or colored pencils, and big match-boxes can be glued together to make miniature chests of drawers.

Cover the matchboxes, or paint them, then stick beads firmly to the front of each drawer, to make handles.

Squeezy dish-washing liquid bottles can be made into good gift containers. Cut off the top and base, so that just the roll is left, and then paint it, cover it in colored paper or leave it plain, rubbing off the printing with a pot scrubber. Cover the roll in paper, trimming the ends so the paper doesn't stick over the end of the roll. Wrap the gift in tissue paper and slide it inside the roll. Cut two circles from the paper, each a little bigger than the ends of the roll,

bend in the edges all around, so the circles fit into the roll, and tuck them in, sticking them with small pieces of transparent tape.

A similar roll, or an empty toilet paper roll, can be made into a cracker. To do this, wrap the roll in two layers of colored crêpe paper, with long ends, tie these long ends with colored ribbon, and fringe the paper.

To make storage boxes to put things in, collect several big cardboard grocery boxes, and cover them in matching or contrasting felt or colored paper. Measure the amount of covering material needed by first drawing in the bottom of the box as it stands on a big sheet of newspaper, then tipping it to one side and drawing around that side. Continue by tipping the box over to the other side to draw that, then standing it on end to draw the ends.

These measurements will give the amount of paper or fabric needed; add an inch or so all around the top of the

paper or fabric, to tuck in.

When the boxes are covered they can be piled in twos along a wall, so they make an open-fronted storage area, or put in a row on the floor. It would be fun to draw parts of an animal on each box so that, when they are put together, the animal is complete.

If a suitable container is not available, it is easy to make a box. Round and square boxes can be made from the same white cardboard. Figure 1 shows you how. Figures 2 and 3 show you how to make a square box. Decide what size your box has to be, then cut out the shape shown on the graph. Cut it from a sheet of white cardboard, glueing the flaps together where indicated.

To cover the box with paper, place the cut-out cardboard shape on the wrong side of a sheet of paper, and draw in pencil the shape shown in figure 2, adding the extra turn-over flaps. Cut out the paper shape and stick it to the box, as shown in figure 4.

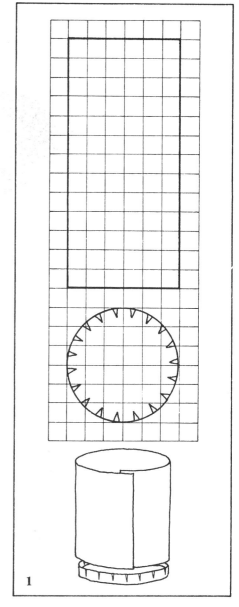

1

**2**

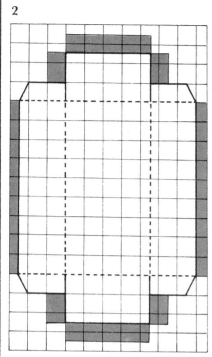

*Cut the box from cardboard, cutting only on the solid lines. Cut the paper to cover it from the bigger pink shape*

**3**

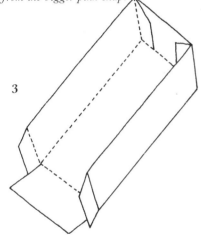

*Fold along the dotted lines to make the box and glue them to secure*

**4**

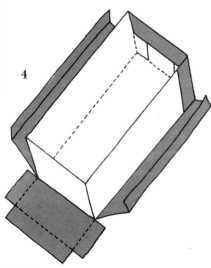

*Fold the paper around the box*

1917

# QUICK MAKE Sunny two-piece

Choose a firm, crease-resistant cotton seersucker for this holiday two-piece and you'll have an adaptable, trouble-free addition to your wardrobe, ideal for both the beach and casual parties. Wear the skirt and halter top together or team the top with plain colored pants or skirts. We have chosen this plaid material in shades of yellow, orange, and red – perfect complements for a suntan.

## You will need:
- ☐ Paper for the pattern
- ☐ 3½ yards 36 inch wide fabric
- ☐ ¾ inch wide elastic to the length of your midriff measurement just under the bust plus 1 inch
- ☐ 4 snap fasteners, small size
- ☐ ¼ yard 1 inch wide belting ribbon
- ☐ One large hook and eye, and one small hook
- ☐ Matching thread

## Pattern
The pattern will fit up to a size 38 inch bust, 40 inch hip. Seam allowances are included.

Make a pattern for the skirt and halter top on paper as shown (**1b**). The skirt is 42 inches long but can be adjusted to any length required.

## Cutting out
Place the pattern pieces on the single fabric as shown in the layout (**1a**). Cut out two skirt pieces (one in reverse), and one top and one lining piece, using the halter top pattern. ½ inch turnings are allowed in the pattern. From single fabric also cut a bias strip (**a**) 2 inches wide for the necktie, and another (**b**) 3 inches wide for the back elastic casing. Cut a waistband (**c**) 4 inches wide to the length of your waist plus ¾ inch for ease and 1 inch for seams.

## Making the two-piece

All seams are stitched with a ½ inch seam allowance unless otherwise stated.

### The halter top
**The midriff strap:** To trim the casing for the midriff strap to the correct length, stretch out the elastic to its full extent, measuring along a tape measure, and trim the casing bias to half the extended elastic length.

Fold the strip in half lengthwise, right sides facing, and stitch ⅝ inch from the edge. Trim seam allowance and turn to right side.

**2.** Insert the elastic through the casing, positioning the casing at the center of the elastic. Stretch the elastic out full, pin the ends of the casing in place, and stitch casing to elastic at each end. By this method the casing will stretch with the elastic.

Overlap the ends of the elastic 1 inch and stitch.

**Making the top: 3.** Turn in ¼ inch double hems along the side edges of both halter top and lining pieces. Then stitch top to lining along the long waist edges, right sides together. Press seam open.

**4.** Turn in the point of both ends of the seam so that the folded edge measures 2¼ inches. Trim the turnings to ½ inch and stitch a ¼ inch double hem. The hemmed ends will become the openings to the lower casing which is stitched later.

**5.** Following the illustration, slip the midriff strap over the lining section as shown. Stitch the halter top to its lining along top edges, right sides together. Press seam open and trim seam allowances.

Turn through to right side and top stitch along top and bottom edges close to seams.

**6.** Position the midriff elastic so that the uncovered part of the elastic is centered at the center front of the halter top, out of sight, between the fabric layers.

Stitch the elastic to the lining only, at the center front, so that it cannot slip out of place when the top is being worn.

Pin and baste 1 inch deep casing along the lower edge of the top to contain the midriff strap. Make sure that the strap is running freely and not caught in with the basting, then stitch the casing. At the top seam edge pin and baste a ½ inch casing. Stitch.

To make the rouleau for the necktie fold the bias strip (**a**) in half lengthwise down the center, right sides facing. Stitch lengthwise. Turn through to right side.

Push in ends and slip stitch to make neat, or knot them firmly and trim. Thread the rouleau through the casing.

Pull the halter top over your head like a sweater. Tie the necktie high or low and arrange the gathers to suit your own figure.

If your bust needs more support, slip a pair of profile forms between top and lining. Baste lightly in place.

### The skirt
Stitch the center back seam, right sides facing. Press seam open.

Pin, baste and stitch darts. Press the front darts toward the front and the back and side darts toward the back.

Pin the skirt around you and adjust the length. Trim the hem allowance to 1½ inches and press. Turn in the raw hem edge narrowly and machine stitch. Finish off the hem.

Turn in each front edge ¾ inch and press. Turn in again ¾ inch and stitch down both edges of the double hem. Gather the top of the skirt to your waist measurement plus ¾ inch. Distribute the gathers evenly.

Pin the skirt waist seam edge to the waistband, right sides together. Position the skirt waist seam 1 inch down from one long edge of the band and with the ½ inch seam allowance at each end of the waistband extending to each side.

Turn in the ends of the waistband ½ inch. Turn in the top edge for 1 inch. Then turn fold over to stitching line. Baste. You now have a finished waistband 1 inch wide with four thicknesses of fabric for support.

Top stitch all around waistband. Attach four snap fasteners at 5 inch intervals down the front of the skirt below the waistband.

**Waistband tab:** Cut a 4½ inch length of 1 inch wide belting for stiffening. Trim the ends into equal points.

**7.** Cut a piece of skirt fabric 5½ inches by 3 inches and place the belting to the wrong side ½ inch from one long edge as shown. Baste.

Fold the fabric in half along the upper edge of the belting, right sides of fabric together. Stitch around both ends, being careful not to stitch through the belting. Trim and turn to right side.

**8.** Turn in remaining seam allowances. Machine stitch all around tab close to the edge.

**9.** Position the tab centrally to the right-hand side of the waistband and stitch in place carefully over the first stitching. Attach two hooks and an eye and hand-work a bar in the position shown to complete the waist edge. (**10**).

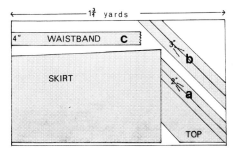

**1a.** *Layout for 36 inch wide fabric*

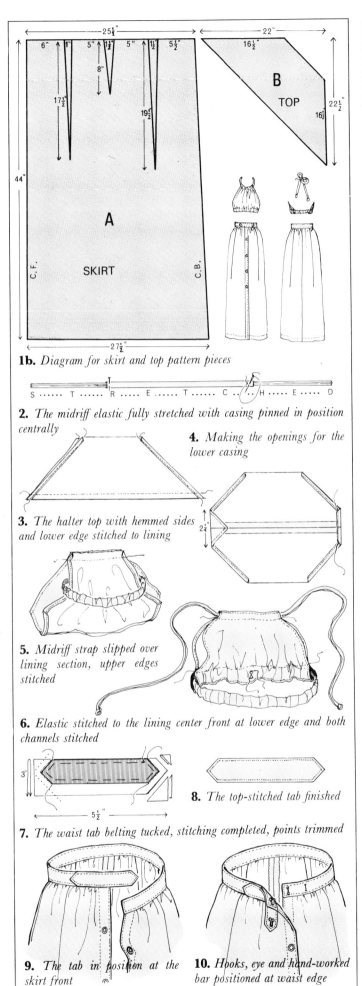

**1b.** *Diagram for skirt and top pattern pieces*

**2.** *The midriff elastic fully stretched with casing pinned in position centrally*

**4.** *Making the openings for the lower casing*

**3.** *The halter top with hemmed sides and lower edge stitched to lining*

**5.** *Midriff strap slipped over lining section, upper edges stitched*

**6.** *Elastic stitched to the lining center front at lower edge and both channels stitched*

**8.** *The top-stitched tab finished*

**7.** *The waist tab belting tucked, stitching completed, points trimmed*

**9.** *The tab in position at the skirt front*

**10.** *Hooks, eye and hand-worked bar positioned at waist edge*

1919

# Cozy quilt

Here's a bright, appealing quilt for a child which is certain to make even naptime seem like a good idea. It's quite a temptation to make, too, as any sewing machine can do the appliqué and quilting required. What lucky child wouldn't consider this the "prize" among his birthday or Christmas gifts?

## To make the quilt

### Materials required for quilt 50 inches by 60 inches

- [ ] 3½ yards blue cotton for backing, 36 inches wide
- [ ] 3 yards Dacron wadding, 36 inches wide
- [ ] ½ yard each of six cotton fabrics (for this quilt: red, pink, blue check, orange check, red flowered dot and red dot)
- [ ] Red and blue thread
- [ ] Tailor's chalk
- [ ] Yardstick
- [ ] Glass-headed pins
- [ ] Tracing paper

### Cutting out the quilt

Cut the blue backing material into two lengths each 1¾ yards long. Placing right sides together, stitch along one long side and press the seam open. Trim backing to 59 inches by 69 inches. Cut the wadding into two 1½ yard lengths and trim each to 50 inches by 30 inches. Lay the 30 inch sides together, making the wadding the same size as the finished quilt, 50 inches by 60 inches. There is no need to baste the two pieces of wadding together as a gentle press with a warm iron will join the fibers. Lay the wadding on the center of the backing, facing the wrong side of this fabric. Baste together (figure 1).

### Cutting out the squares and motifs

Using the various cotton fabrics that you have chosen – bright prints are

Continued on page 18

▼ One of the motifs used to decorate the quilt

# TRACING PATTERNS FOR BEDSPREAD MOTIFS

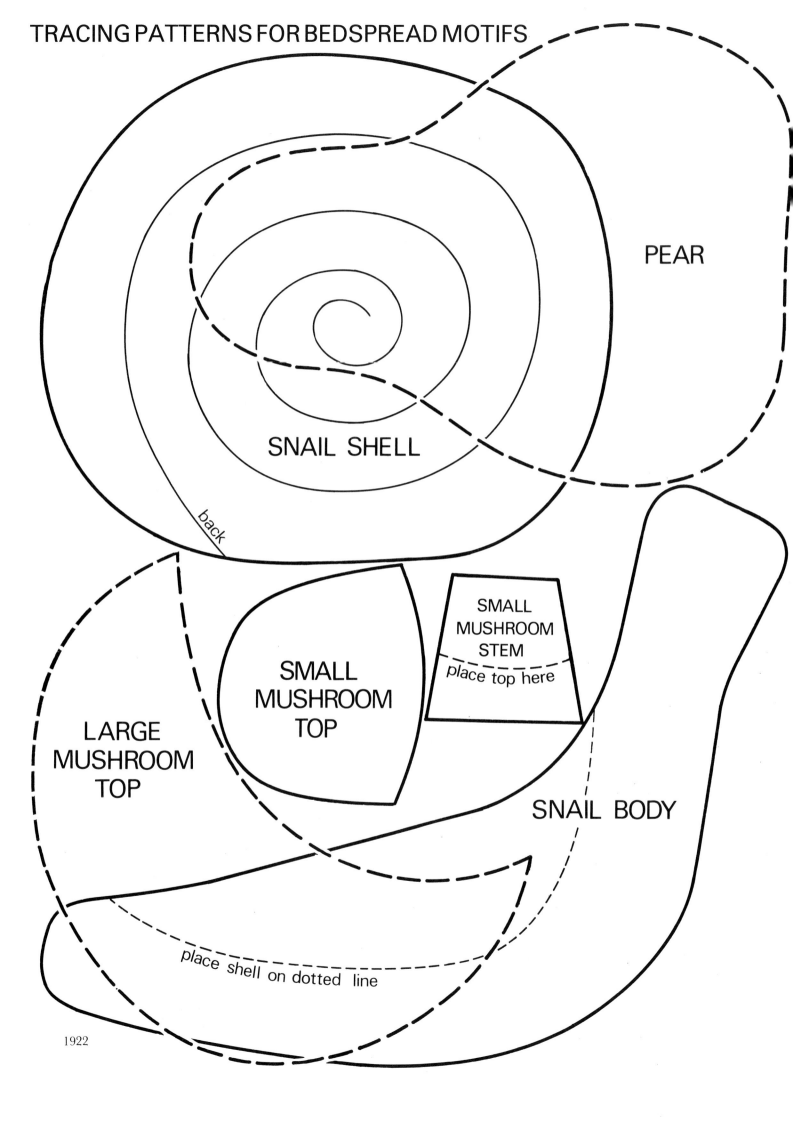

PEAR

SNAIL SHELL

back

SMALL MUSHROOM STEM

place top here

SMALL MUSHROOM TOP

LARGE MUSHROOM TOP

SNAIL BODY

place shell on dotted line

1922

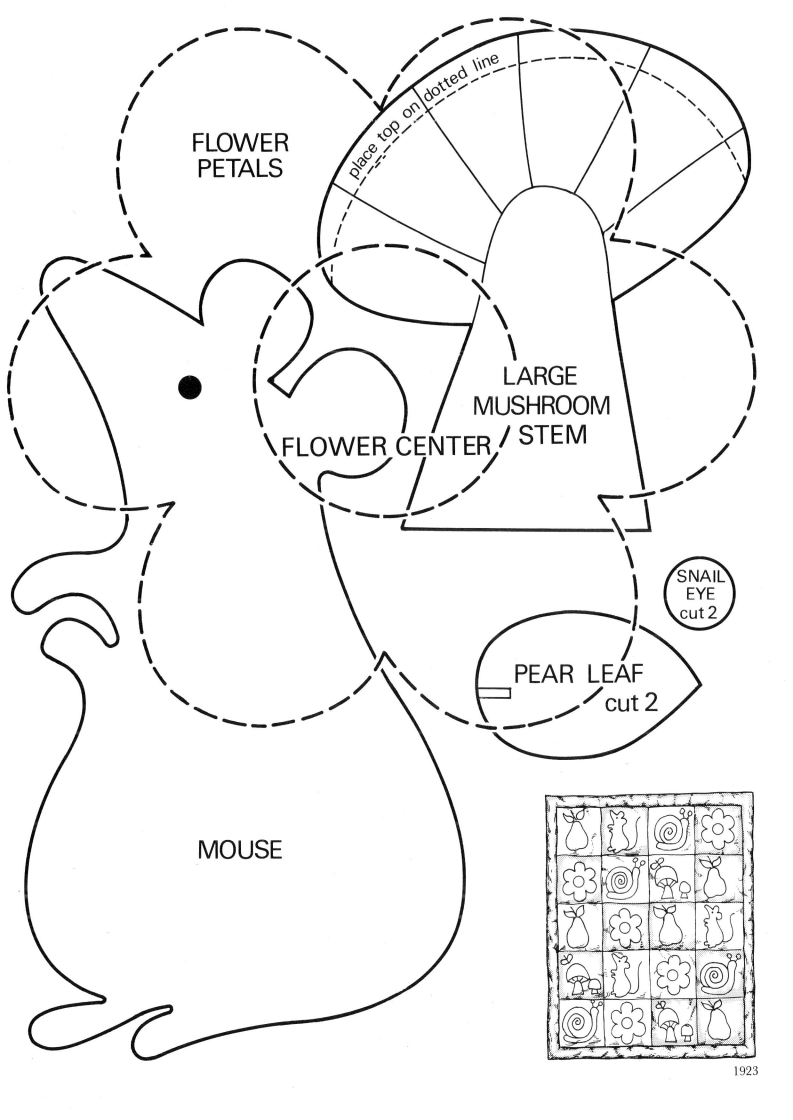

FLOWER PETALS

place top on dotted line

FLOWER CENTER

LARGE MUSHROOM STEM

SNAIL EYE
cut 2

PEAR LEAF
cut 2

MOUSE

1923

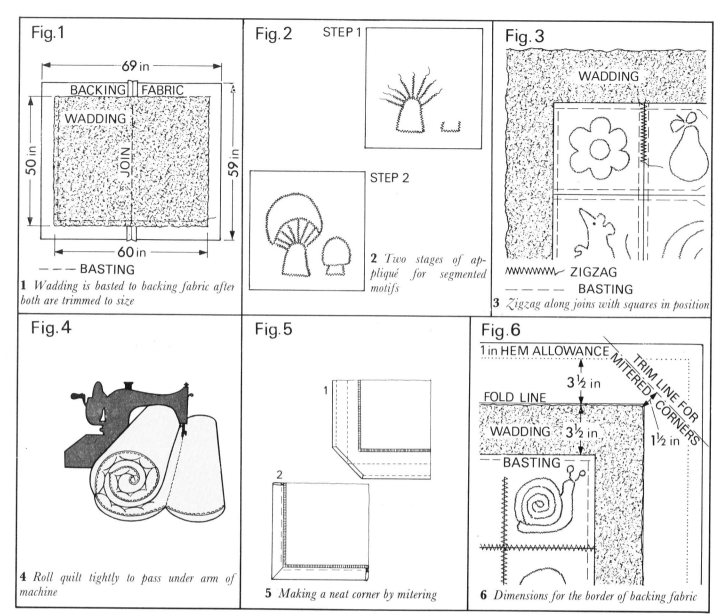

**Fig. 1**

69 in
BACKING | FABRIC
WADDING
JOIN
50 in
59 in
60 in
– – – BASTING

**1** *Wadding is basted to backing fabric after both are trimmed to size*

**Fig. 2**

STEP 1

STEP 2

**2** *Two stages of appliqué for segmented motifs*

**Fig. 3**

WADDING

www — ZIGZAG
– – – – – BASTING

**3** *Zigzag along joins with squares in position*

**Fig. 4**

**4** *Roll quilt tightly to pass under arm of machine*

**Fig. 5**

1

2

**5** *Making a neat corner by mitering*

**Fig. 6**

1 in HEM ALLOWANCE
TRIM LINE FOR MITERED CORNERS
3½ in
FOLD LINE
WADDING 3½ in
1½ in
BASTING

**6** *Dimensions for the border of backing fabric*

cheerful – plan an arrangement of these which will harmonize and balance well. Cut into twenty 12 inch squares; this dimension will include a $\frac{3}{4}$ inch seam allowance.

Using the tracing pattern for the motifs, trace each separately onto tracing paper and cut out. Cut out twenty motifs from the various fabrics, remembering that no seam allowance is required for these as the pieces are sewn along the rough edge with zigzag stitch.

**Sewing on the motifs**

Baste one motif in the center of each square and, placing a sheet of thin paper under the square to keep the material from puckering, machine stitch along the edge of the motifs using zigzag stitch. (Do not use this supplementary layer of paper when quilting; this applies only to appliqué.) When using one section of the motif over another (e.g. the mushroom), first baste and stitch the lower part onto the square, then baste and stitch the upper part on (figure 2).

Tear away the paper from the under side of the stitching and press each square with a damp cloth.

**Stitching the quilt together**

Machine stitch the squares together, using a $\frac{3}{4}$ inch seam allowance. When this has been completed, the joined squares will number four on one side and five on the other. Press the seams open. Lay the joined squares onto the wadding, right side up. Pin these layers together and baste around the edges, then baste around the sides of each machine stitched square. This will hold the squares in position when the machine quilting of each section is done.

Stitch along the joins between the squares, using the fancy stitch of your choice. A fairly open stitch will probably create the best effect and contrasts nicely with the zigzag used for appliqué (figure 3).

To avoid difficulty in passing the bulk of the quilt under the arm of the machine while stitching, roll it up tightly and have someone help you hold it as you stitch (figure 4).

**Finishing the edges**

Trim the corner of the backing fabric as indicated, then miter and baste (figure 5). Turn the excess backing material which extends beyond the rim of wadding over to the front of the quilt to form a border (figure 6). Allow 1 inch turning and baste. Machine stitch along the joining of border edge and appliqué squares, and stitch again around the outside edge of the border, $\frac{1}{4}$ inch from the folded edge.

Tidy up the back of the quilt by trimming machine threads and remove basting stitches.

*Note:* When making quilts, use glass-headed pins. Count out the number you need before starting to work and again after removing them, to make quite certain that none is left in the work. Use only one needle, and be very careful not to lose it.

# TOYS

This startled little lion, in plaid cotton squares, makes an attractive toy. He's quick and easy to make with a thick upholstery fringe for a mane and a purchased tassel for a really lion-like tail. He's a toy to delight any child.

**You will need:**

☐ Scraps of plaid cotton fabric
☐ Two circles of light lavender denim, each $\frac{3}{4}$ inch in diameter, for outer eyes
☐ Two black and white buttons, each $\frac{1}{2}$ inch in diameter, for inner eyes
☐ One circle of pink felt a fraction less than $\frac{3}{4}$ inch in diameter, trimmed as in the picture, for nose
☐ One circle of deep pink felt, same size as nose, for mouth
☐ Matching sewing thread
☐ Fabric adhesive
☐ 36 inches of 3 inch deep, thick brown fringe, for mane
☐ One brown purchased tassel, for tail
☐ Kapok
☐ Black heavy-duty cotton thread

**Making patchwork pieces for lion**

Make a paper pattern from the graph, in which one square represents 1 inch. Seam allowances of $\frac{1}{4}$ inch are included. Cut the plaid cotton fabric into squares and divide them into three piles, one for each side of lion and one for gusset. See that the colors are evenly divided.

Baste and machine stitch the patches together to produce two pieces, each 12 inches by $10\frac{1}{2}$ inches and one long strip, 49 inches by 3 inches, for gusset.

Using the paper pattern, cut out the two body sides from the patchwork. Using $\frac{1}{4}$ inch seams, baste and machine stitch the gusset to the two body pieces, right sides facing. Start at end of back, where tail is to go. Leave the short gusset seam open for turning. Turn to right side and stuff tightly, pushing the kapok well down into the base of the legs. Stitch up back leg, using small hemstitches. Insert the purchased tassel, for the tail, at the top. Stitch gusset to secure tail in place.

**To make mane**

Using matching thread, stitch thick brown fringe all around head (see picture), working all around the head twice and finishing off at the chin.

**Features**

Using fabric or latex adhesive, stick lavender denim and black and white buttons in position on lion for eyes. Glue pink felt in position for nose, and deep pink felt for mouth.

Using heavy-duty black cotton thread, work the nose marks in outline stitch. Make tiny stitches on the nose and several large loops each side for whiskers, knotting firmly. Cut ends of the loops.

Graph for Patchwork Lion

One square = 1 sq. in.

# The luxury look

This dainty mohair blouse has a luxurious and expensive feel to it. It looks good teamed with a silky shirt, but can also be worn on its own.

## Sizes

Directions are for 32in bust. The figures in brackets [ ] refer to the 34, 36 and 38in sizes respectively.
Length to shoulder, 18¾[19: 19½:19¾]in.

### Gauge
7 sts and 9 rows to 1in over st st worked on No. 3 needles.

## Materials

Reynolds Wendy Whisper 7 [8:8:9] 25 grm. balls
One pair No. 2 needles (or Canadian No. 11)
One pair No. 3 needles (or Canadian No. 10)
7 buttons

## Back

Using No. 2 needles, cast on 95[101:107:113] sts.
**1st row** K2, *P1, K1, rep from * to last st, K1.
**2nd row** *K1, P1, rep from * to last st, K1.
Rep 1st and 2nd rows 16 times more.
Change to No. 3 needles.
Change to st st.
Beg with a K row, work 4 rows st st.

## Shape sides

Inc one st at each end of next and every following 6th row until there are 115[121: 127:133] sts.
Continue without shaping until work measures 12[12: 12½:12½]in from beg, ending with a P row.

### Shape armholes
Bind off 5[5:7:7] sts at beg of next 2 rows.
Dec one st at each end of every row until 95[97:99: 105] sts rem, then at each end of every other row until 85[87:89:93] sts rem.
Continue without shaping until armholes measure 6¾[7: 7:7¼]in from beg, ending with a P row.

### Shape shoulders and back neck
**Next row** Bind off 4[4:5:5] sts, K17[17:17:18] sts, bind off 43[45:45:47] sts, K to end.
Complete this side first.
**1st row** Bind off 4[4:5:5] sts, P to last 2 sts, P2 tog.
**2nd row** K2 tog, K to end.
**3rd row** Bind off 4 sts, P to last 2 sts, P2 tog.
Rep 2nd and 3rd rows once more.
Work 1 row. Bind off rem 4[4:4:5] sts.
With WS facing, attach yarn to rem sts.
**1st row** P2 tog, P to end.
**2nd row** Bind off 4 sts, K to last 2 sts, K2 tog.
Rep 1st and 2nd rows once more, then 1st row once.
Bind off rem 4[4:4:5] sts.

## Left front

Using No. 2 needles, cast on 45[49:51:55] sts.
Work 34 rows rib as given for Back.
Change to No. 3 needles and st st. Beg with a K row, continue in st st, dec one st in center of first row on 34in size only. 45[48:51:55] sts.
Work 4 rows.

### Shape side
Inc one st at side edge on next and every following 6th row until there are 55[59:61: 65] sts.
Continue without shaping until work measures same as Back to underarm, ending at side edge.

### Shape armhole
Bind off 5[5:7:7] sts at beg of next row.
Work 1 row.
Dec one st at armhole edge on every row until 45[46:47: 49] sts rem, then at each end every other row until 40[41: 42:44] sts rem.
Continue without shaping until armhole measures 2½[2¾:2¾:3]in from beg, ending at center front edge.

### Shape neck
**Next row** Bind off 6[7:7:8] sts, work to end.
Dec one st at neck edge on every row until 23[23:24:25] sts rem, then on every other row until 16[16:17:18] sts rem.
Continue without shaping until armhole measures same as Back to shoulder, ending at armhole edge.

### Shape shoulder
Bind off at arm edge every other row 4[4:5:5] sts once, 4 sts twice and 4[4:4: 5] sts once.

## Right front

Work as given for Left front, reversing all shaping.

## Sleeves

Using No. 2 needles, cast on 111[111:121:121] sts.
Work in garter st for 5 rows.
Change to No. 3 needles.
Commence patt.
**1st row** K1, * ytf, K3, sl 1, K2 tog, psso, K3, ytf, K1, rep from * to end.
**2nd row** P.
**3rd row** P1, *K1, ytf, K2, sl 1, K2 tog, psso, K2, ytf, K1, P1, rep from * to end.
**4th row** K1, *P9, K1, rep from * to end.
**5th row** P1, *K2, ytf, K1, sl 1, K2 tog, psso, K1, ytf, K2, P1, rep from * to end.
**6th row** As 4th.
**7th row** P1, *K3, ytf, sl 1, K2 tog, psso, ytf, K3, P1, rep from * to end.
**8th row** P.
These 8 rows form patt.
Keeping patt correct, dec one st at each end of next 10 rows.

Bind off 5 sts at beg of next 14 rows.
Bind off rem 21 [21:31:31] sts.

## Neck border

Join shoulder seams.
Using No. 2 needles and with RS facing, pick up and K 43[44:44:45] sts along right front neck, 59[61:61: 63] sts along back neck edge and 43[44:44:45] sts down left front neck edge.
**1st row** *K1, P1, rep from * to last st, K1.
**2nd row** K2, *P1, K1, rep from * to last st, K1.
Rep 1st and 2nd rows 3 times more, then 1st row once. Bind off in rib.

## Right front border

Using No. 2 needles, cast on 8 sts.
**Next row** K2, (K into front, then into back of next st, K1) 3 times. 11 sts.
Beg with a 2nd row, work in rib as given for Neck border.
Work 2 rows.
**Next row** (buttonhole row) Rib 4 sts, bind off 2 sts, rib to end.
**Next row** Rib to end, casting on 2 sts above those bound-off on previous row.
Work 22 rows rib.
Make buttonhole as before on next 2 rows.
Make 5 more buttonholes with 22 rows between each.
Work 4 rows after last buttonhole has been completed.
Bind off in ribbing.

## Left front border

Work as given for Right front border, omitting buttonholes.

## Finishing

Press each piece lightly under a damp cloth with a warm iron.
Join side seams. Sew in sleeves, gathering sleeves slightly on each side of shoulder seam, noting that the whole of the sleeve is sewn into armhole including first 8 rows.
Sew borders to fronts. Press seams. Sew on buttons.

1927

# Smart ways with smocking

▲ *Smocking on bodice combines trellis stitch and feather stitch*

No other form of embroidery is quite so simple yet effective – hence the enduring popularity of smocking. Through the combined devices of gathering into pleats and subsequent decorative stitching, the appearance of the fabric's surface and of the whole garment is altered in the most attractive way.

Originally used to control fullness in (and even to help waterproof) farm workers' and shepherds' heavy garments, smocking has evolved as a decorative means of transforming a full range of babies', children's and adult garments. Any garment with fullness to be gathered in may be worked in this way, using either a few rows or wide bands of smocking. Some of the possibilities for blouses and smocks are illustrated here, showing some areas which lend themselves particularly well to this form of decorative embroidery.

**Fabrics for smocking**
The best background for smocking is a smooth, even-textured fabric: cotton, silk, cotton and wool mixtures or fine woolens are all suitable. The work is

▲ *A long panel on a bodice*

▲ *Traditional-look smocking*

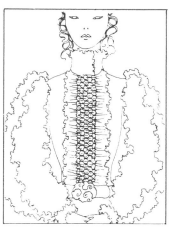

▲ *Smocking gathers a frill*

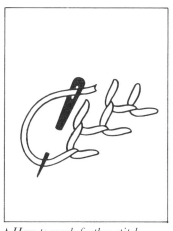

▲ *How to work feather stitch*

done on the material before the garment is finished. Allow about three times the required finished length, as it is particularly important not to skimp on material; this factor is crucial to the effectiveness of a piece of work.

## Color possibilities

As the decorative value of smocking does not depend on the color – too much color actually detracts from the effect of the stitching – plan ahead to make quite certain that the color scheme is kept simple. There are three possibilities to consider when smocking: one may use threads in the same color as the background fabric, threads in a contrasting color, or threads of various colors. The effectiveness of both matching and contrasting threads is exemplified by the two blouses illustrated. On the pink blouse, a little color has been introduced with some floral embroidery on the bodice, whereas the smocking itself is merely a part of the textured backdrop. Conversely, on the green bodice, colored threads draw particular attention to the smocked areas.

## Stitches and threads

Many different stitches are used in smocking, including variations on outline stitch, chevron and feather stitch. Coton à broder and Pearl cotton are particularly suitable threads for this type of stitchery, as they are strong and will not twist (as is sometimes the case with 6-strand floss).

## Smocking transfers

Before smocking, the area to be worked on must be marked out with rows of dots. As this marking must be very accurate, the use of a transfer for smocking dots will prove invaluable. Transfers are available in various gauges: the spacing of the dots required depends on the weight of the material used and the smocking design itself.

▲ *Surface honeycomb stitch reduces fullness at waist and upper sleeve*

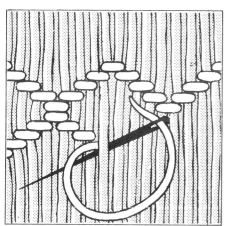

▲ *Trellis stitch*

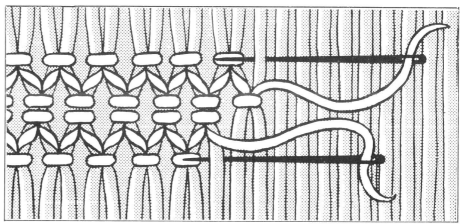

▲ *Surface honeycomb stitch. The thread remains on the right side of the work*

1930

# Multi-colored afghan

Worked in glowing russet tones, this afghan has a warm and welcoming look. Use it as a car rug, as a blanket or as a specially beautiful beadspread. It can be worked in other color schemes to compliment wherever it is used.

**Size**

About 52in by 60in.

**Gauge**

One motif measures about 4in diameter.

**Materials**

3-ply Fingering Yarn
1 oz. skeins
1 skein dark brown, A
5 skeins medium brown, B
5 skeins rust, C
5 skeins orange, D
5 skeins gold, E
1 No. D (3.00 mm) crochet hook

## Motif

Using No. D hook, ch4.
Join with ss to form a ring.
**1st round** Ch3, 11dc into ring, ss to ch3.
**2nd round** Ch3, 1dc in same place as ss, *ch2, 2dc into next dc, rep from * to end, finishing with ch2, ss to 3rd of ch3.
**3rd round** Ch3, 2dc in first ch2 space, *ch2, 1dc in same space, yoh, insert hook in same space, yoh and draw through 2 loops, yoh and draw through rem 3 loops – called 2dc tog – 1dc in same space, rep from * to end, finishing with ch2, 1dc in

▲ *Close-up detail of the motif, actual size*　　　▼ *Chart showing the position of the motifs and colors*

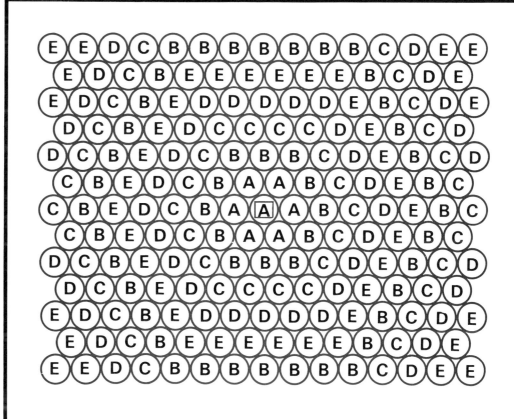

same space, ss to 3rd of ch3.
**4th round** *Ch1, 5dc in space, ch1, 1sc into 2dc tog, rep from * to end, finishing with a ss into a ss of previous round. Fasten off.
Make 7 motifs in dark brown, 48 in medium brown, 44 in rust, 44 in orange and 46 in gold.

## Finishing

Using one dark brown motif as the center, position the other six around it and sew together, joining 2 shells of the center motif edge to each of the 6 motifs.
Sew 12 medium brown motifs around these and so on, following the chart.
Press with a warm iron over a damp cloth.

# Windfall of wildflowers

The soft colors and delicate shapes of wildflowers are not easy to reproduce, but these panels, worked in cross-stitch, have captured their freshness and charm. They would be perfect as a set of floral pictures – perhaps for a dining room or bedroom wall – or the panels could be mounted onto pillows, with one color from the embroidery picked out for the binding or piped edge. Natural-colored evenweave linen makes a good background to work on, but a more vivid shade of woolen fabric could be chosen to complement the color scheme of one particular room.

A chart for one of the six designs is given here. Others will follow in later volumes. You might like to consider working the panels as individual gift items—the designs combine nature's own colors and will appeal to both traditional and modern tastes.

## Materials required to make each panel measuring 15½ inches by 25½ inches:

☐ ⅝ yard evenweave linen (20 threads to the inch, 54 inches wide, ivory)
☐ Crewel needle, size 8 or 9
☐ Hardboard or softboard measuring 15½ inches by 25½ inches
☐ Unbleached muslin or plain cotton for backing measuring 15½ inches by 25½ inches
☐ D.M.C. 6-strand floss in the following colors:

### Dandelion panel

White, black, 762 gray, 640 linen, 435 snuff brown, 976 chestnut, 938 peat, 725 amber gold, 922 light terra cotta, 355 dark terra cotta, 949 geranium, 734 muscat green, 319 forest green, 3346 almond green, 470 moss green

## To work cross-stitch

The key word in working cross-stitches is regularity: each cross-stitch should make a perfect square, being worked down and across over an equal number of threads of an evenweave fabric. For these panels, use three strands of floss in the needle, working each stitch over two threads of evenweave linen.

The main point to remember is that in whichever direction you work the stitch, the upper stitches must always lie in the same direction (usually from bottom left to top right). If they do not, they will reflect the light differently from the

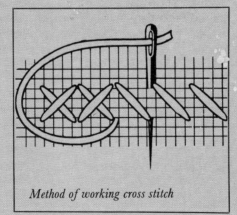

*Method of working cross stitch*

other stitches and will stand out clearly as mistakes.

The most even finish for filling in large areas of color is obtained by working a row of diagonal stitches (half cross-stitches) in one direction and then completing the stitches by working another row in the opposite direction. If you are working a complete design in cross-stitch, keep the texture even by working the whole design in half cross-stitch and

then complete the stitches in the other direction. This also helps to build up the design very quickly. If there is only a small area to cover, it is possible to use the alternative method in which one stitch is completed at a time, but this will look less even.

## Mounting the finished work

Mount the completed panel on a piece of masonite or plywood cut exactly to the required finished size of the panel. Lay the piece of board centrally over the back of the work and with fine string (or very strong thread), lace the fabric – not too near the edge – at the back from side to side and then from top to bottom. Pull the lacing firmly until the work is evenly stretched without being puckered. Secure the lacing thread ends by knotting several times.

Make the back of the work neat by stitching the unbleached muslin or other cotton over it to conceal the lacing. Simply take the piece of backing fabric, turn under edges ½ inch all around, baste, then slip stitch firmly in place to cover the lacing. Remove the basting. This method of mounting is suitable for most forms of embroidery, and you can then frame the embroidery if you wish. Alternatively, stitch two plastic curtain rings to the back of the work on either side and about halfway between to hold a cord for hanging the panel on the wall.

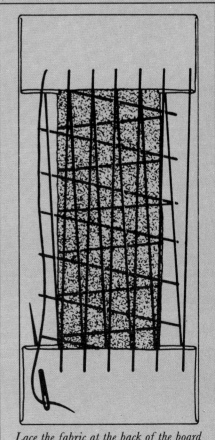

*Lace the fabric at the back of the board*

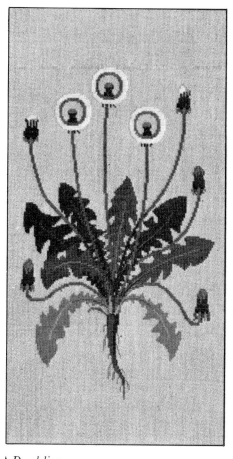

▲ *Dandelion*

▲ *European elder*

▲*Wild parsnip*

▼ *Groundsel*

▼ *Nettle*

▼ *Tansy*

1933

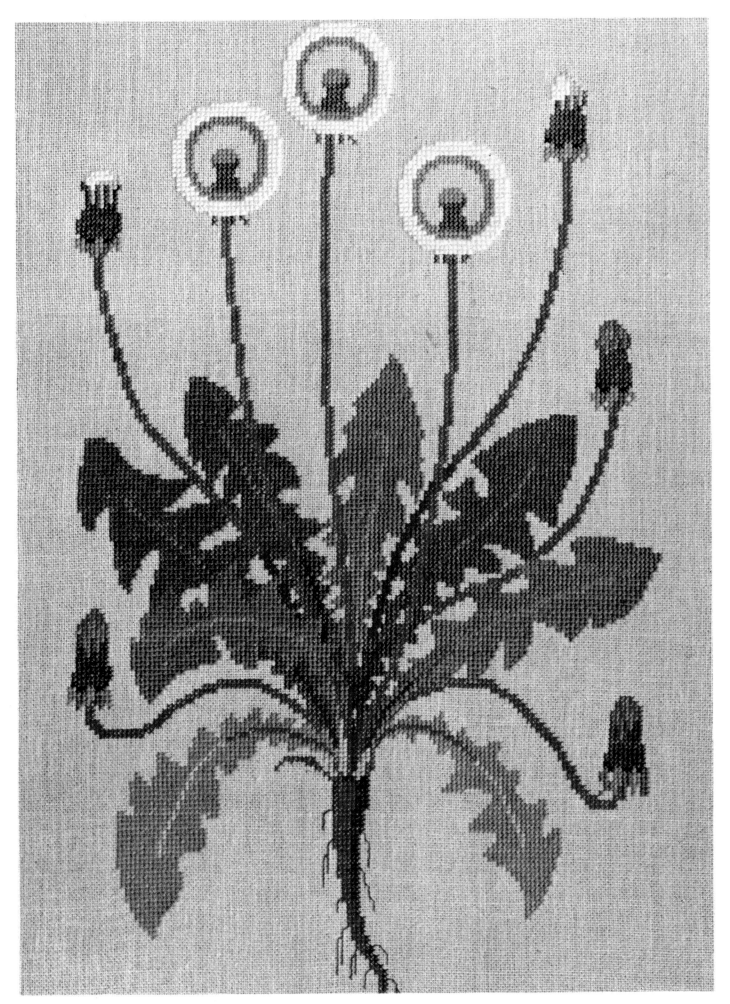

1934

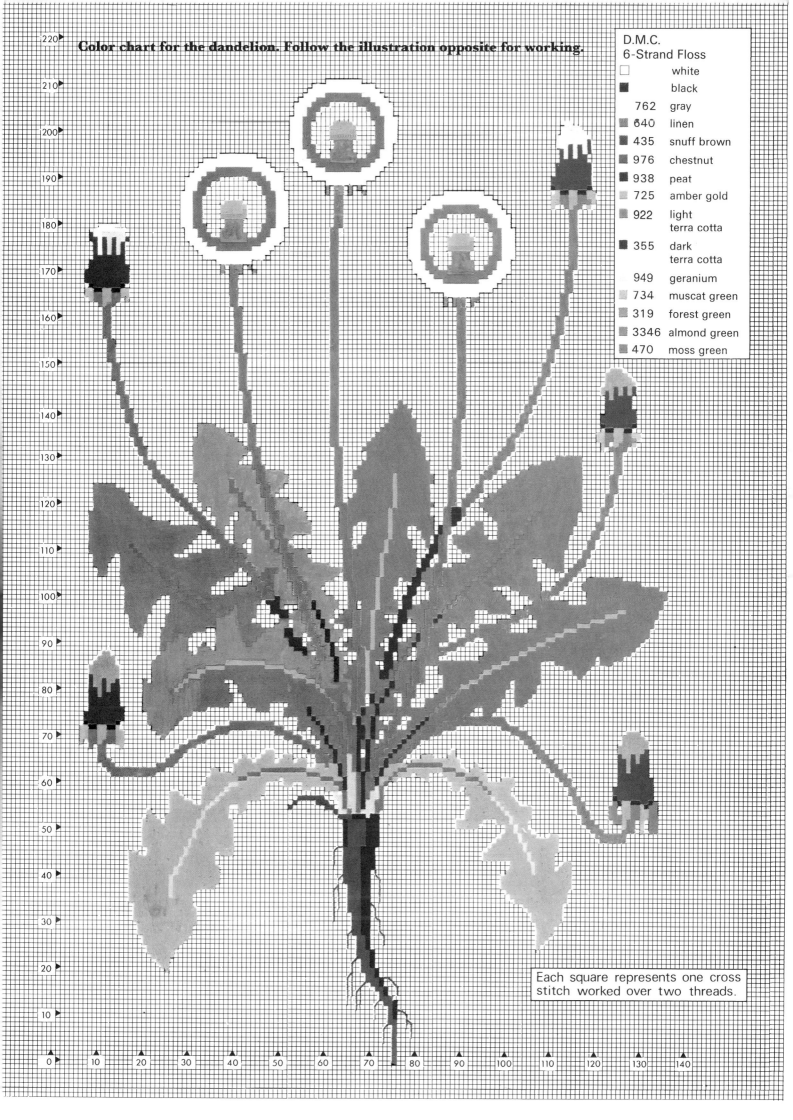

**Color chart for the dandelion. Follow the illustration opposite for working.**

D.M.C.
6-Strand Floss

| | | |
|---|---|---|
| | | white |
| | | black |
| | 762 | gray |
| | 640 | linen |
| | 435 | snuff brown |
| | 976 | chestnut |
| | 938 | peat |
| | 725 | amber gold |
| | 922 | light terra cotta |
| | 355 | dark terra cotta |
| | 949 | geranium |
| | 734 | muscat green |
| | 319 | forest green |
| | 3346 | almond green |
| | 470 | moss green |

Each square represents one cross stitch worked over two threads.

# Classic crew neck

A heavily textured pattern gives a rugged masculine look to this classic sweater.

## Sizes

Directions are for 38in chest. The figures in brackets [] refer to the 40 and 42in sizes respectively.
Length to shoulder, 26[27:28]in, adjustable.
Sleeve seam, 17½[18:18½]in, adjustable.

## Gauge

9 sts and 14 rows to 2in over patt worked on No. 7 needles using yarn double.

## Materials

Bucilla Winsom
18 [19:20] 2 oz. skeins
One pair No. 5 needles (or Canadian No. 8)
One pair No. 7 needles (or Canadian No. 6)
Set of 4 No. 5 double-pointed needles
**NB** Yarn is used double throughout

## Back

Using No. 5 needles and 2 strands of yarn, cast on 90[90:98] sts.
**1st row** K2, *P2, K2, rep from * to end.
**2nd row** P2, *K2, P2, rep from * to end.
Rep these 2 rows for 2in, ending with a 2nd row.
Change to No. 7 needles. Commence patt.
**1st row** K2, *P6, K2, rep from * to end.

**2nd row** P2, *K6, P2, rep from * to end.
**3rd row** As 2nd.
**4th row** As 1st.
**5th row** As 1st.
**6th row** As 2nd.
**7th row** K.
**8th row** P.
**9th row** P4, *K2, P6, rep from * to last 6 sts, K2, P4.
**10th row** K4, *P2, K6, rep from * to last 6 sts, P2, K4.
**11th row** As 10th.
**12th and 13th rows** As 9th.
**14th row** As 10th.
**15th row** K.
**16th row** P.
These 16 rows form patt. Continue in patt until work measures 18[18½:19]in from beg, or desired length to underarm ending with a WS row.

## Shape armholes

Keeping patt correct, bind off 4[2:4] sts at beg of next 2 rows. 82[86:90] sts.
**Bind off 2 sts at beg of next 4 rows.
K2 tog at each end of next and every other row until 66[68:70] sts rem.**
Continue without shaping until armholes measure 8[8½:9]in from beg, ending with a WS row.

## Shape neck and shoulders

**Next row** Patt 26[27:27], turn and slip rem sts on holder.
**Next row** Bind off 3 sts, patt to end.
**Next row** Bind off 4 sts, patt to end.
Rep last 2 rows twice more.

Work 1 row. Bind off rem 5[6:6] sts.
With RS facing, slip first 14[14:16] sts on holder and leave for back neck, attach yarn to rem sts and patt to end.
Complete to correspond to first side, reversing shaping.

## Front

Using No. 5 needles and 2 strands of yarn, cast on 90[98:98] sts.
Work as given for Back until work measures same as Back to underarm, ending with a WS row.

With RS facing, slip first 8[8:10] sts on holder and leave for center neck, attach yarn to rem sts and patt to end. Complete to correspond to first side reversing shaping.

## Sleeves

Using No. 5 needles and 2 strands of yarn, cast on 42[42:50] sts.
Work in rib as given for Back for 2in, ending with a 2nd row.
Change to No. 7 needles. Work in patt as given for Back, inc one st at each end of 9th (1st:9th) and every following 10th row until there are 62[66:70] sts.
Continue without shaping until sleeve measures 17½[18: 18½]in from beg, or desired length to underarm ending with a WS row.

### Shape top
Bind off 4 sts at beg of next 2 rows.
Dec one st at each end of next and every other row until 26 sts rem.
Bind off 2 sts at beg of next 6 rows and 3 sts at beg of next 2 rows.
Bind off rem 8 sts.

## Neckband

Join shoulder seams.
Using set of 4 No. 5 needles, 2 strands of yarn and with RS facing, pick up and K 13 sts down side of back neck K across back neck sts, pick up and K 13 sts up other side of back neck and 24 sts down side of front neck, K across front neck sts, then pick up and K 24 sts up other side of front neck. 96[96:100] sts.
Continue in rounds of K2, P2 rib for 3in.
Bind off loosely in rib.

## Finishing

Sew in sleeves.
Join side and sleeve seams.
Fold neckband in half to WS and slip stitch in place.
Press seams very lightly under a damp cloth with a cool iron, being careful not to flatten patt.

### Shape armholes
Bind off 4[6:4] sts at beg of next 2 rows. 82[86:90] sts.
Work as given for Back from ** to **.
Continue without shaping until armholes measure 6[6½: 7]in from beg, ending with a WS row.

### Shape neck
**Next row** Patt 29[30:30], turn and slip rem sts on holder.
Bind off at neck edge every other row 3 sts twice and 2 sts twice.
K2 tog at neck edge on next and following alt row.

Continue without shaping until armhole measures same as Back to shoulder, ending with a WS row.

### Shape shoulder
Bind off at arm edge every other row 4 sts 3 times and 5[6:6] sts once.

*▲ This delightful beach basket and pair of summer sandals can be made from just over 1lb of raffia*

# CRAFTS

# string along with raffia

Raffia work, in the pleasing natural material, can be used to make any number of attractive and useful items, from table mats to sandals. There are several different ways of using raffia; it makes a brilliant embroidery thread; it can be wound and woven over a cardboard base, it can be woven to produce a piece of fabric. It can also be coiled and twisted around thick sisal string to make a really firm structure, such as the beach basket shown here. Raffia work is a fascinating craft—and it's ideal to take along for something to do on a holiday—light, easy to carry, and very relaxing once you've mastered the basic techniques. You could start by making table mats in easy single and double stitch, and go on to make our basket and sandals.

Raffia, the immature leaf of the African palm, comes mostly from Malagasy and natural, dry raffia is essential for this kind of work. Prepared raffia is glycerined and the moisture it contains reduces the tautness of the finished work, making it look and feel limp. Natural raffia is sold in hanks of **varying sizes, and is bought by the pound weight.**

For the beginner, sisal string is the best foundation on which to coil the raffia—3-ply is a good thickness. Cane of the cheapest quality can be used in place of sisal, but if it is used, do not soak it with water as you would for cane work.

It is important that the hairs of the sisal do not show through between the raffia coils; they should be smoothed down during working and the sisal string can be pulled through a piece of beeswax first, which will help to keep the hairs down. If a few do show when the work is finished, they can be cut off, but it would be a long, tedious job to cut off many.

## Tools

A needle with a large eye and a blunt point (a No. 14 tapestry needle is ideal) and a pair of scissors are all the tools needed for raffia work.

## Methods of working

Begin by working a coil for the foundation row.

Cut sisal string diagonally for about 1 inch, making a kind of point to reduce thickness in the finished join when the end is tucked in. Run string through beeswax, to reduce the number of hairs that stand up. Thread needle with enough strands of raffia to equal the thickness of one ply of the sisal string.

Using your left forefinger and thumb, hold both the cut end of sisal string and one end of the raffia, leaving the other end of raffia, with the needle attached, hanging free (diagram **1**).

With the right forefinger and thumb, hold only the raffia, still leaving needle hanging free. The raffia, now held with the right forefinger and thumb, is in position to coil onto the sisal string to make the foundation row (referred to from now on as "the row below") (diagram **2**).

To do this, proceed as follows:

Using your right forefinger and thumb, twist the raffia evenly for about 1 inch, then coil that twisted raffia, working away from you, around the sisal string, as if you were turning the handle of a sewing machine. Thus you will get a good, even tension. Twist another inch of raffia and coil that around, keeping the raffia taut all the time to stop it unwinding. Continue covering the sisal string with twisted raffia, bending the string to form a circle.

## To join

Tuck the end of the sisal into the first one or two coils and resume coiling until the whole ring is completely covered (diagram **3**).

The foundation row or the "row below" is now completely covered with twisted raffia. Continue to cover the sisal string with the twisted raffia for six or eight coils; this is the beginning of your second circle. You can continue to work in circles, to make a table mat, as shown in diagrams **4** and **5**, in which single and double stitches are used.

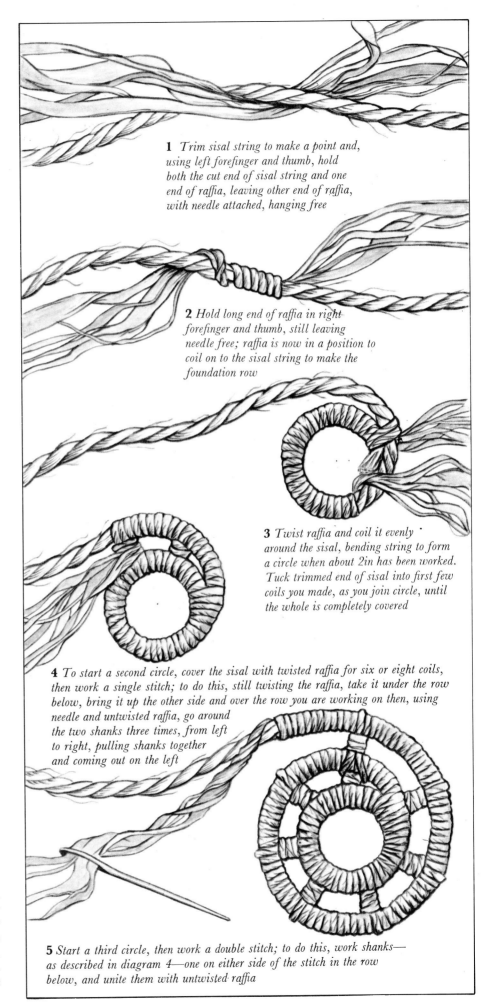

**1** *Trim sisal string to make a point and, using left forefinger and thumb, hold both the cut end of sisal string and one end of raffia, leaving other end of raffia, with needle attached, hanging free*

**2** *Hold long end of raffia in right forefinger and thumb, still leaving needle free; raffia is now in a position to coil on to the sisal string to make the foundation row*

**3** *Twist raffia and coil it evenly around the sisal, bending string to form a circle when about 2in has been worked. Tuck trimmed end of sisal into first few coils you made, as you join circle, until the whole is completely covered*

**4** *To start a second circle, cover the sisal with twisted raffia for six or eight coils, then work a single stitch; to do this, still twisting the raffia, take it under the row below, bring it up the other side and over the row you are working on then, using needle and untwisted raffia, go around the two shanks three times, from left to right, pulling shanks together and coming out on the left*

**5** *Start a third circle, then work a double stitch; to do this, work shanks— as described in diagram 4—one on either side of the stitch in the row below, and unite them with untwisted raffia*

## Single stitch

To make a single stitch for connecting your second row to your first row, still twisting the raffia, take it into the row below, bring it up to the other side and over the row you have started to work. The needle now comes into use for uniting the two shanks of raffia.

Take the raffia (not twisted) and the needle around the two shanks, from left to right, pulling shanks tightly together so they meet. Meanwhile, with the left forefinger and thumb, hold the row you are working and the row below, so that a flat shape is achieved. Go around the shanks twice more with untwisted raffia. Be sure always to come out on the left-hand side, so the work will look the same on both sides.

## Double Stitch

This is made by forming shanks, as for the single stitch, one on either side of the stitch in the row below, and then united by untwisted raffia.

## Treble Stitch

To form a treble stitch, the row below must have two stitches close together. Make the shanks of the first stitch to the right of the two stitches below; make the second between the two stitches, and the third on the left of the two stitches. Unite these three shanks as the double stitch, using untwisted raffia.

When you have mastered these basic stitches, you will be able to design your own work, or make our beach basket and sandals.

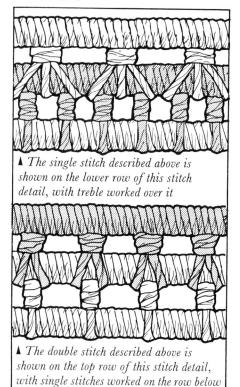

▲ *The single stitch described above is shown on the lower row of this stitch detail, with treble worked over it*

▲ *The double stitch described above is shown on the top row of this stitch detail, with single stitches worked on the row below*

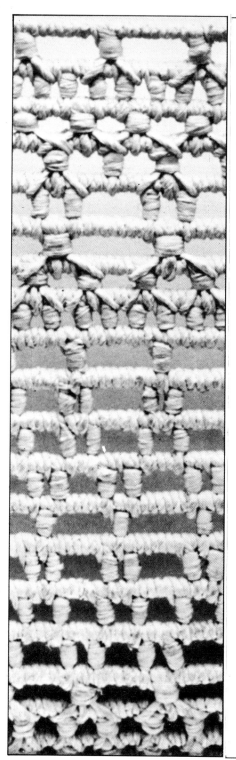

*For the basket sides, work as follows:*
*1st row:* Work single stitches into the string, working 7 stitches to ✳ every 3in✳
*2nd row:* Work one double stitch into each single stitch in row below
*3rd row:* Work one treble stitch into each two double stitches below
*4th row:* Work single stitches into row below, two stitches over each treble
*5th row:* Work in single stitch, one stitch to either side of two single stitches in row below
*6th row:* Work two single stitches inside every two stitches in row below
*7th row:* Work one single stitch between each two in row below
*8th row:* Work one single stitch either side of single stitches in row below
*9th row:* Work two single stitches between groups of two stitches in row below
*10th row:* Work single stitches in groups of two between groups of two in row below
*11th row:* Work one single stitch into center of each two in row below
*12th row:* Work three single stitches between each stitch in row below
*13th row:* Work one treble stitch over every two stitches in row below
*14th row:* Work one treble over every two treble stitches in row below
*15th row:* Work one single stitch either side of each treble in row below
*16th row:* Work one treble over each two singles in row below, and one single between each treble
*17th row:* Work two trebles over every three trebles in row below
*18th row:* Work two singles between each treble of row below
*19th row:* Work one double stitch over two single stitches in row below, leaving one single stitch free between each double
*Now work handles:* directions are given right

## Beach basket

### You will need
- [ ] 1 lb natural, dry raffia
- [ ] Sisal string
- [ ] Beeswax
- [ ] One hank soft white garden string
- [ ] 2 No. 12 or 14 tapestry needles
- [ ] Scissors
- [ ] A plywood basket base, ready bored, available in different shapes and sizes from craft shops

### To prepare the basket base
Using the string and the two tapestry needles, thread string both ways through each hole on plywood base, threading needles and string opposite ways through one hole and working all the way around, so both sides of plywood are completely threaded. Finish by tying a neat knot on the one side and work on this side, so the raffia work hides the knot.

### Working the pattern
Follow the detail photograph of the basket's side for the pattern but, if you prefer, work out a random pattern of your own. Our basket measures approx-

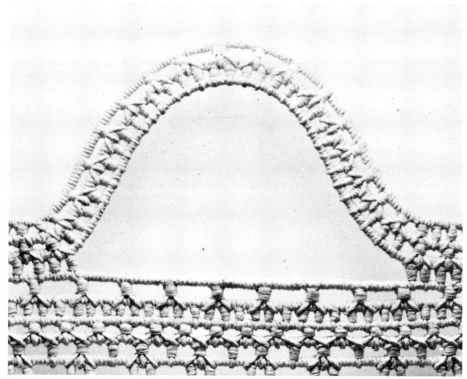

*▲ A detail of the basket handles, for which full directions are given, below*
*▼ Make a pair of sandals to this design quickly and easily from the directions, right*

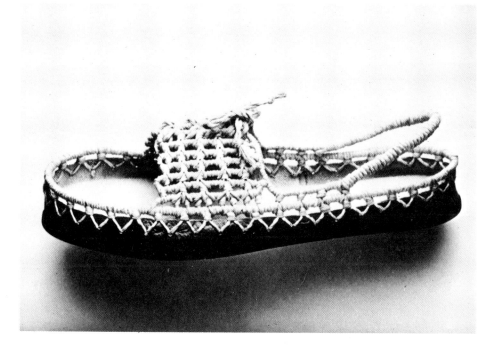

## Sandals

### You will need
- ☐ ½oz natural dry raffia
- ☐ Sisal string
- ☐ Beeswax
- ☐ Pair of moccasin bases, ready bored
- ☐ No. 12 or 14 tapestry needle
- ☐ Scissors

Work a row of double stitches into all the holes on the moccasin bases, working right shank of a stitch into same hole as left shank of last stitch made, for the welt. Place your foot into moccasin and mark where the heel strap is to join to main part of sandal and where the uppers are to be placed.

### Left foot
Starting on outside left of the weft where the upper begins, nearest the toes, work toward heel, as follows:

*1st row:* 8 single stitches, for 2¾ inches, then bend sisal back toward toe, as shown in the illustration.

*2nd row:* Work 1 double stitch, 3 treble stitches and 1 double.

*3rd row:* Bend sisal back toward heel and work 1 single and 4 double stitches.

*4th row:* Bending sisal toward toe again, work a row of five double stitches.

*5th row:* Bending sisal back over work, make 1 single and 4 double stitches.

*6th row:* Bending sisal, work 1 single and 4 double stitches.

*7th row:* Bending sisal, work 1 single and 4 double stitches.

Bending sisal over outside edge of heel side of upper, work a single stitch into top end loop, then a double stitch into top end loop and second loop, then a single stitch into second loop, and a single into third loop of flap. Make four double stitches into side of sandal, having by this time gone around back edge of flap. When first heel strap position is reached, make a thick coil, using sisal and raffia, joining again with another double at the other heel strap position. Work other side of upper in the same way.

Make right foot sandal to match.

Braid two strands of raffia for ties, thread them through the holes and then knot the ends to secure.

Both the sandals and the basket can be worked in different colored strands of raffia, to give an exciting contrast. Natural colored raffia can be dyed at home, using any ordinary household boiling dye. This produces lovely pastel shades which are fast dyed. Try the sandal ties in two colors and natural—red and blue, perhaps—for a trim.

imately 9 inches deep by 19½ inches wide.

### The handles
When the sides have been worked, mark out a space 7 inches wide in the center of the top row on both sides, using pieces of contrasting thread.

Work a row of single stitches into the row below, working three single stitches to 1 inch, starting from one left-hand piece of marker thread and working around to the opposite marker thread on the other side of basket.

Wind twisted raffia around the sisal for 11½ inches and then, leaving this 11½ inches free for the handle, work single stitches into row below, exactly as before. When the marker thread on the opposite side is reached, wind twisted raffia around sisal for 11½ inches and then work a row of treble stitch, making 3 treble stitches to every 2 inches all around basket, working each treble stitch over two shanks of the row below. When the prepared handle sections are reached, work single stitches. Work a final row, working single stitches between double stitches: 3 double stitches and 2 single stitches to 1 inch. Work treble stitches over handles.

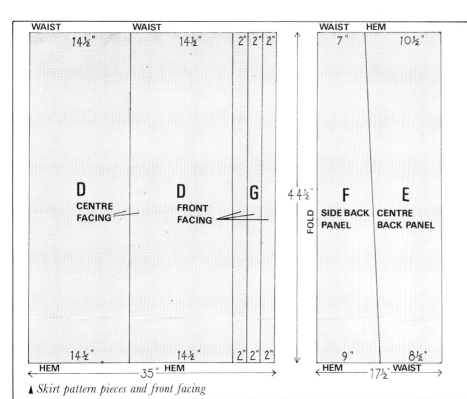

*Skirt pattern pieces and front facing*

# Glamorous batwing

This glamorous batwing dress has been made up in a semi-transparent cotton voile, but it would look equally charming in a warm, light-weight wool fabric. It's a garment for all kinds of occasions; wear it for a dinner party, an informal evening at home or even as a housecoat.

If a semi-transparent fabric is used, a few basic rules must be observed when making it: seams and hems must be very narrow, turnings must be trimmed or concealed and all linings, bindings, elastic and tapes must be as near flesh colored as possible.

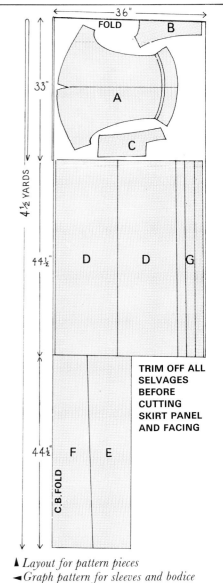

TRIM OFF ALL SELVAGES BEFORE CUTTING SKIRT PANEL AND FACING

*Layout for pattern pieces*
◄ *Graph pattern for sleeves and bodice*

1942

1943

# Glamorous batwing

## Making the pattern

Make a paper pattern from the graph pattern (1 square represents 1 inch), and transfer all markings. Allow $\frac{1}{2}$ inch seam allowance all around when cutting out and a $\frac{1}{2}$ inch hem. There are 5 pattern pieces.

1 – Bodice front (cut 2)
2 – Bodice back (cut 1)
3 – Sleeves (cut 2)
4 – Skirt (cut 5)
5 – Front facing

## Materials you will need:

☐ 4$\frac{1}{2}$ yards 36 inch wide fabric with all-over design
☐ $\frac{1}{2}$ yard fine cotton lining if a voile or similar fabric is being used for the dress, flesh colored or toning with the dress fabric
☐ 1 yard cotton bias binding
☐ $\frac{1}{2}$ yard $\frac{1}{4}$ inch wide elastic
☐ 1 yard $\frac{3}{4}$ inch elastic
☐ 3 yards 1 inch seam binding
☐ **10 gripper fasteners**
☐ Matching thread, fine gauge
☐ 2 yards rick rack braid
☐ Small hook and eye

**1.** Cut two strips of bias binding and baste to the wrong side of the sleeves, 3$\frac{1}{4}$ inches from the wrist edge.

Machine stitch both edges of the binding to form a channel. Cut two lengths of elastic to the wrist measurement plus 1 inch and thread them through the channel, stitch to secure the elastic at both ends.

Right sides facing, lay the bodice fronts and bodice back on the lining pieces and baste, then stitch around the neckline edges. Trim turnings to $\frac{1}{4}$ inch, clip into the curve, turn to right side and press.

Baste and then stitch all around these bodice pieces on the right side, $\frac{3}{8}$ inch from the raw edge. (These stitches can be removed when they are no longer required.)

**2.** Baste and sew sleeve darts. Press flat.

**3.** Join front and back bodice pieces at the shoulders, using French seams.

**4.** Join sleeves to bodice, matching shoulder seams to sleeve darts, and easing in fullness evenly. Trim and make turnings neat. Press toward bodice.

**5.** Top stitch rick rack braid to cover the sleeve joins.

**6.** Close sleeve underarms with narrow French seams, closely trimming and clipping the curve after the first stitching.

**7.** Make a narrow double hem on the wrist edges of the sleeves. Stitch.

**8.** Join the five sections of the skirt together using narrow French seams.

Run two parallel lines of gathers around the skirt waist, one 1$\frac{1}{2}$ inches from the edge, the second $\frac{1}{2}$ inch from the edge. Draw up to fit the bodice waist measurement and secure threads by winding around pins. Mark a seamline on the bodice 1$\frac{1}{2}$ inches from the edge with a line of basting.

**9.** Stitch the top gathering line on the skirt to this line, matching side and side-back seams, wrong sides facing.

**10.** On the right side of the garment, press the skirt down into position and top stitch the bodice seamline, close to the previous line. Turn up $\frac{1}{2}$ inch on the waist edge of the bodice, baste this to the second, lower line of gathering and top stitch in position.

**11.** Thread the $\frac{3}{4}$ inch wide elastic through the channel, arranging gathers at the side sections, rather than at back and front. Try the garment on, adjust the elastic for comfortable fit and pin at the waist front edges. Trim off the surplus. Hold the gathers in place with a few stitches.

Check the hem length, turn up a narrow double hem. Stitch.

**12.** Join the front facing strips and then cut the lengths to fit the center front edges, plus 1 inch for turnings.

Right sides facing, baste and then stitch the facings to the dress, $\frac{1}{2}$ inch from the edge. Press facing over turnings.

On the wrong side of the work, lay a length of seam binding along facing seam line and top stitch close to the binding edge.

Turn in, and press the $\frac{1}{2}$ inch seam allowance of the facing under the free edge of the binding. Top stitch in position. Press, baste and top stitch a narrow double hem at top and bottom of facings.

Fold facings in and catch stitch from neckline to waist and at the hem.

Insert fasteners from neck to just below the knee. If you find difficulty in inserting a gripper fastener through the elastic at the waistline, arrange the fasteners so that they fall just above and just below the waist, securing the waist opening with hooks and eyes or a trouser waist fastening.

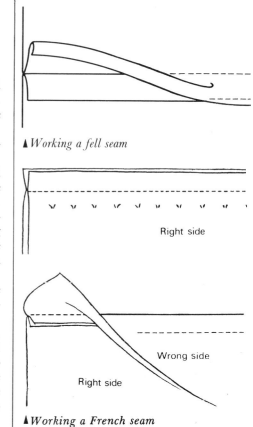

▲ *Working a fell seam*

▲ *Working a French seam*

▲ *The dress can be cut short to wear as a light cover-up for the beach*

**8**

**9 - 10**

**11**

**12**

Stitch here to hold gathers

Stitch along this line

**13**

a

b

c

d

*▲ Cotton fabric lined with waterproof material makes pretty shower curtains*

# Curtain linings and interlinings

Professionally made lined and interlined curtains are expensive to buy, so it is a useful accomplishment to be able to make them at home. Making good curtains is not difficult, and with a little care really good results can be achieved.

## Choosing the fabric

Choose the best quality fabric you can afford for your curtains, bearing in mind the aspect of the room and the existing color scheme. Next to the carpet, curtains give the largest amount of color and texture to a room so it is essential that the right fabric is chosen. Remember when choosing curtain material that some fabrics drape better than others. Always ask to see the fabric draped before you buy it—it can look very different lying flat on a counter. Check, too, whether the fabric is washable or needs dry-cleaning, whether it is shrink resistant and whether it will fade if exposed to strong sunlight.

Large abstract and geometric patterns are usually too overpowering for the average living room and if a patterned fabric is used it should be of a small design and in keeping with the size of the room. More fabric will be needed if it is patterned. A large pattern repeat can be expensive too; extra material must be allowed for matching the pattern and there is often some wastage.

Make quite sure that the pattern is printed correctly on the grain of the fabric as otherwise this can present problems when making the curtains.

## Linings and Interlinings

### Linings

Linings are used in curtains for several reasons:

▲ *Properly lined, curtains will drape softly and evenly*

**a.** A lining helps a curtain to drape better.

**b.** A lining protects the curtain fabric from sun and light, and also from dust and dirt which damage the curtain fabric and make it wear out more quickly.

**c.** A lining can act as an insulator if a metal insulated lining called Milium is used. Milium will also make a curtain draft proof and is therefore particularly useful when used to curtain a door. Cotton sateen is normally used for lining curtains. This fabric is usually 48 inches wide and the colors most often used are fawn and white. Although cotton sateen does come in various colors, it is desirable to line all the curtains in the house with the same color, if possible, to give a uniform effect from the outside of the house. An exception must be made for curtains with a white background where a matching white lining is more suitable.

## Interlinings

It greatly improves the appearance of most curtains if they are interlined. This makes them drape better and shows off the texture or pattern of the fabric to best advantage. Interlining gives a curtain a padded luxurious look and is certainly well worth the extra trouble involved.

Any firmly woven, soft fabric such as cotton flannel can be used for interlining curtains. The main thing to consider is that the material you use is a good insulator and that the interlining material is not so expensive that the cost of making the curtains becomes too high.

Interlined curtains are very expensive if made professionally. All the work is done by hand and this adds considerably to the cost.

## Detachable linings

It is now possible to make curtains with detachable linings. This makes it possible to wash or dry-clean the linings separately, which is quite useful as they often seem to need cleaning before the curtains do.

When a detachable lining is used the curtains and linings are made separately but are attached to the same hooks.

Although detachable linings are very useful in some rooms they do not have quite the professional finish of hand made lined curtains. These have the linings stitched to the curtain around the two sides and bottom. An attached lining prevents dirt and dust from getting in between the curtain and lining fabric, giving more protection to the curtain fabric and making it last longer.

## Measuring and cutting curtain fabric

Measure the window and track carefully with a wooden yardstick. A yardstick is invaluable when making curtains because an accurate measurement can not be obtained with a tape measure.

Curtains should either hang to the sill, 2 to 4 inches below the sill or to the floor. Never use in-between measurements as they will look out of proportion. Floor length curtains should hang to within $\frac{1}{2}$ inch of the floor.

Allow $1\frac{1}{2}$ to 2 times the width of the track for a standard heading, but allow 2 to $2\frac{1}{2}$ times the width of the track if using a fancy heading such as a Deep Pleat heading.

For top and bottom hems, allow 6 to 8 inch turnings altogether. More fabric must be allowed if a pattern has to be matched, and it is advisable to allow one pattern repeat on each curtain for this purpose.

To get a straight line for cutting draw a thread if possible. If a pattern happens to be badly printed and is not printed on the grain of the fabric, cut to the pattern and not to the thread. Plain material should always be cut to the grain.

Place the fabric on a large table, preferably rectangular, with the selvage running down the longer edge of the table. The edges of the table can then be used to square up the curtains if a thread cannot be drawn.

Cut out each curtain, being careful to match patterns where necessary.

Cut off all selvages as this prevents the curtains from puckering.

If it is necessary to join widths of fabric together, the join should come at the sides of the window. Use a plain seam and press it open.

## Making a lined curtain

### Cutting the lining

Do not try to draw a thread on lining sateen, but square it up on a table or use a triangle.

Cut off all selvages.

Cut the lining the same size as the curtain fabric, joining if necessary. Make a plain seam, with right sides facing, and press open.

### Preparing the curtains

**1.** Turn in $1\frac{1}{2}$ inches at sides and bottom of the curtain fabric.

**2.** Miter the two bottom corners.

**3.** Using matching thread, serge around sides and bottom of curtain.

## Locking in the lining

A lining is locked to the curtain fabric to prevent the lining falling away from the top fabric when the curtain is hanging.

First place the curtain on a table with the wrong side uppermost. Lay the lining on top of the curtain, wrong sides together. The raw edges of the lining should be flush with the curtain all around, so trim the sides and the lower edge by the required amount.

**4.** Fold back the lining at the center of the curtain and lock lining to curtain as shown. Make long loose stitches to avoid puckering. The locking should start and end 6 to 8 inches from both top and bottom.

To help you work the stitches in a straight line you may find it helpful to make a crease mark on the lining with your thumb.

Locking is usually worked at 12 inch intervals across a curtain. So in a curtain 48 inches wide there would be three rows of locking, one down the middle of the curtain and one to each side 12 inches in from the edge.

**5.** When the locking is completed, fold in lining at sides and bottom of curtain for 1 inch, mitering corners. Baste.

Make a line of basting stitches across the curtain 6 inches from the top. This is to keep the lining firmly in place until the heading tape is attached.

Slip stitch lining to curtain around the two sides and bottom of curtain using matching thread and leaving about 6 inches unattached at the top.

## Making interlined curtains

### Cutting the interlining

The interlining fabric is cut to the size of the finished curtain. It is taken to the edge of the curtain and extends up to the top under the heading tape. This means that the interlining should be cut 3 inches narrower than the curtain fabric to allow the edges of the curtain to be turned over $1\frac{1}{2}$ inches.

**6.** If a join needs to be made in the interlining, a lap seam should be used. As soft fabric tends to stretch it is advisable to stitch with two rows of zigzag machine stitching. Alternatively the lapped seam can be sewn by hand. Position the interlining on the curtain $1\frac{1}{2}$ inches up from the lower edge and $1\frac{1}{2}$ inches in from both sides. Lock the interlining to curtain fabric in the same way as the lining was locked to the curtain (see figure **4**).

**7.** Turn in the sides and lower edge $1\frac{1}{2}$ inches, catch stitch curtain to interlining. Attach the lining as before but this time lock the lining to the interlining fabric.

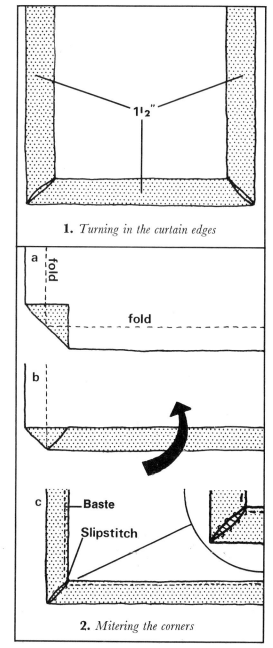

**1.** *Turning in the curtain edges*

**2.** *Mitering the corners*

## Curtain headings

### Choice of heading

There are so many different types of curtain track and heading tape available that it is advisable to give your curtain headings some thought and to decide on the effect required. Decorative curtain poles are very much in fashion again and can look most attractive used with pleated or deeply gathered heading tapes.

Many different effects can be achieved by using the new tracks and headings and it is advisable to find a home furnishing department or hardware store which displays some of them.

If a lined or interlined curtain is being used, make sure when choosing a track that it is strong enough to take the weight. Interlining adds considerably to the weight of a curtain.

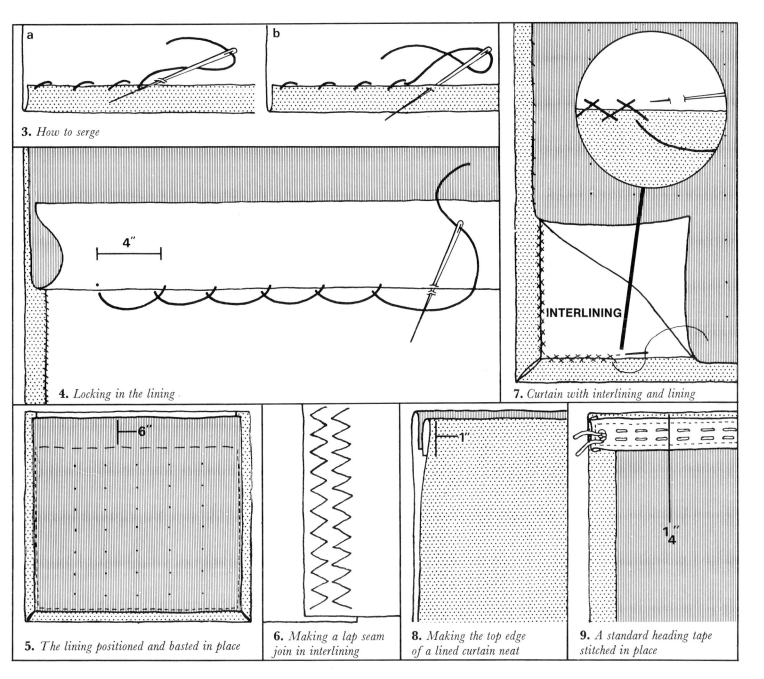

**3.** *How to serge*

**4.** *Locking in the lining*

**7.** *Curtain with interlining and lining*

INTERLINING

**5.** *The lining positioned and basted in place*

**6.** *Making a lap seam join in interlining*

**8.** *Making the top edge of a lined curtain neat*

**9.** *A standard heading tape stitched in place*

**Tapes and hooks**

Here are some of the most widely used heading tapes:

☐ Standard heading tape; this is a 1 inch wide tape for even gathering on all types of fabrics where a simple gathered heading is required. The tape has two woven-in cords for drawing up the fullness.

☐ Easy pleating tape: these are for making pinch pleats easily. No cord is used for drawing up the tapes, but special deep pleat hooks are required and the pleated effect is achieved by inserting the prongs of the hooks in the pockets on the tape. Single, double or triple pleats can be made.

When using the tapes it is necessary to work out carefully the quantity of fabric required and the number of sets of pleats in each curtain. Generally, however, the amount required is between two and three times the finished curtain width but it pays to measure carefully to avoid wasting expensive materials.

☐ For special headings, especially for sheers, use an all-purpose crinoline fabric. Alternatively, use Pellon with soft edges which makes it ideal for use with glass fibers. All of these come in a variety of widths which can be pleated as desired into a variety of styles ranging from simple pencil pleats to the more complicated triple pinch or box pleated designs.

Various detailed leaflets are available on these and other heading styles and can be obtained from most home furnishing counters at department stores or other stores with notions counters.

**Applying standard heading tape**

Size up curtains to obtain the correct length of tape required. Don't forget to use a wooden yardstick for this.

Trim the top edge of the curtain, leaving about 1 to 2 inches for turnings.

**8.** Turn in top of curtain and lining 1 to 2 inches as shown. Cut the heading tape to curtain width plus 1 inch.

**9.** Position and baste heading tape to top of curtain, turning $\frac{1}{2}$ inch under at each end.

Pull out the cords from turned in ends. Machine stitch along top and bottom of tape and along the two sides, taking care not to catch in the cords.

Tie the cords at one end and draw up the cord at other end to the required width. Do not cut off the cord but wind it on to a cord tidy for a neat finish. The cords can then be released easily for dry cleaning or washing.

Press curtains, insert hooks and the curtains are ready for hanging and enhancing your home.

# Ties to knit and crochet

Here are three quick-to-make neckties, two knitted with crochet edges, the third worked entirely in crochet. If you choose the colors carefully to go with shirts and suits, they should be gifts that any man would be pleased to receive. Worked in multi-color yarn, the final effect of each tie will be different every time you work the pattern – that's the fun of multi-colored yarns. The ties can be worked in solid colored yarn if you prefer a more formal accessory. Choose an interchangeable yarn, but make absolutely certain the gauge is the same.

Knit some now for those hard-to-fill family Christmas stockings!

## Sizes

**Bobble-stitch tie.** 2¼in wide at lower edge by 49in long when pressed

**Garter-stitch tie.** 2¼in wide at lower edge by 55in long when pressed

**Tubular tie.** 2¼in wide at lower edge by 51in long when pressed

### Gauge

**Bobble-stitch tie.** 4 sts and 2 rows to 1in over dc worked on No.F hook.

**Garter-stitch tie.** 5½ sts and 10 rows to 1in over garter st worked on No.5 needles.

**Tubular tie.** 7½ sts and 9½ rows to 1in over st st worked on No.3 needles.

## Materials

**Bobble-stitch tie.**
Variegated Sports Yarn
2 ounces main color, A
1 ounce solid contrast color, B
One No. F (4.00 mm) crochet hook
One No. E (3.50 mm) crochet hook

**Garter-stitch tie.**
Variegated Sports Yarn
2 ounces main color, A
1 ounce solid contrast color, B
One pair No. 5 needles (or Canadian No. 8)
One No. E (3.50 mm) crochet hook

**Tubular tie.**
Variegated Sports Yarn
2 ounces main color, A
1 ounce solid contrast color, B
One pair No. 3 needles (or Canadian No. 10)
One No. C (2.50 mm) crochet hook

## Bobble-stitch tie

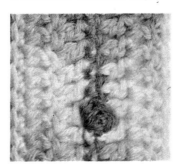

Using No.F hook and A, ch201.

**1st row** (WS) Into 2nd ch from hook work 1hdc, work 1hdc into each of next 53ch, 1sc into each of next 50ch, 1hdc into each of next 10ch, 1dc into each of next 85ch. Turn.

**2nd row** Ch3 to count as first dc, work 1dc into each of next 89 sts, 1hdc into each of next 5 sts, 1sc into each of next 50 sts, 1hdc into each of next 5 sts, 1dc into each st to end. Turn.

**3rd row** Ch2 to count as first sc, work 1sc into each of next 121 sts, *(yrh, insert hook into next st and draw up loop, yrh and draw through 2 loops) 3 times into same st, yrh and draw through 4 loops on hook, ss into same st – called bobble 1 –, 1sc into each of next 5sc, rep from * to end. Turn.

**4th row** As 2nd.

**5th row** As 1st but beg by working ch2, 1hdc into each of next 54 sts. Fasten off.

### Edging

Using No.E hook and B, with RS facing work 1 row sc around all edges, working 3sc into each corner st. Join with ss to first sc. Fasten off.

## Garter-stitch tie

Using No.5 needles and A, cast on 250 sts.
Work in garter st for 5 rows.

### Shape wide end

| | |
|---|---|
| **1st row** | K110, turn. |
| **2nd row** | Sl 1P, K to end. |
| **3rd row** | K100, turn. |
| **4th row** | Sl 1P, K to end. |
| **5th row** | K90, turn. |
| **6th row** | Sl 1P, K to end. |
| **7th row** | As 3rd. |
| **8th row** | As 2nd. |
| **9th row** | As 1st. |
| **10th row** | As 2nd. |
| **11th row** | K. |

### Shape narrow end

| | |
|---|---|
| **1st row** | K70, turn. |
| **2nd row** | Sl 1P, K to end. |
| **3rd row** | K60, turn. |
| **4th row** | As 2nd. |
| **5th row** | As 1st. |
| **6th row** | As 2nd. |

Work in garter st for 5 rows. Bind off loosely K-wise.

### Edging

Work as given for Bobble-stitch tie.

## Tubular tie

Using No.3 needles and A, cast on 24 sts.

**1st row** *K1, ytf, sl 1P, ytb, rep from * to end. This row forms patt and is rep throughout.

Continue in patt until work measures 26in from beg.

### Shape neckband

**Next row** K3 tog, *ytf, sl 1P, ytb, K1, rep from * to last 3 sts, ytf, P3 tog.

Work 7 rows patt without shaping.

Rep last 8 rows once more, then first of them again. 12 sts.

Continue without shaping until work measures 41in from beg.

### Shape end

**Next row** Inc in first st, patt to last st, inc in last st.

**Next row** *Sl 1P, ytb, K1, ytf, rep from * to end.

Rep last row 6 times more.

**Next row** Inc in first st, patt to last st, inc in last st. 16 sts.

Rep 1st patt row until work measures 55in from beg, allowing 4in to be taken up by edging.

Weave sts tog or divide sts onto 2 needles and bind off tog.

### Edging

Using No.C hook, B and with RS facing, work 1 row sc around all edges, working 3sc into each corner st and 1sc into every other row along side edge. Join with ss to first sc. Fasten off.

## Finishing

**For all ties.** Run in ends. Press under a damp cloth using a warm iron.

1951

strips (d) each 12 inches by 1 inch, for armhole binding, and one strip (e) 6 inches by 1 inch, for pocket binding.

## Making the apron

With right sides together, pin and baste armhole binding to each armhole edge, from A to B. Stitch, taking ¼ inch seam. Turn binding to wrong side, turn in long raw edge for ¼ inch and slip stitch in place (figure 1).

**Neck casing.** Trim armhole binding at the top even with the top of the apron. To make neck casing turn under edge for ¼ inch, then turn under again for 1 inch. Stitch close to fold.

Join two short ends of two of the tie strips together, right sides facing, and machine stitch, taking ½ inch seam. Place the long sides of the joined strip together, right side facing, and machine stitch, taking ¼ inch seam.

Using a large safety pin attached to one end of strip, turn strip to right side, turn in ends and slip stitch to make neat.

Using a safety pin attached to one end of tie strip, thread the tie through the casing at the top of the apron.

Make the waist tie strip as above, using the two remaining strips of fabric.

To make the waist casing, turn in each long edge of the casing strip ⅜ inch and press. Position the casing on wrong side of apron, wrong sides facing and baste. Machine stitch casing to apron close to each fold. Remove basting, then thread the tie strip through.

### The pocket

Run a gathering thread through the top of the pocket, ¼ inch in. Pull up till top of pocket measures 6 inches. Secure gathering thread and bind top of pocket in the same way as armholes, leaving ends of binding raw. Turn in ½ inch seam allowance on remaining edges of pocket, and baste.

Pin the pocket in position indicated on graph. Baste, then machine stitch down close to the edge, leaving top open.

### The frill

Join the frill together down two selvage edges, right sides together, taking a ¼ inch seam. Press seam open. Pin, baste and sew a ¼ inch hem along one long edge. Run a gathering thread along the unhemmed long edge, ¼ inch in, and pull up till frill fits apron hem. Secure gathering thread, and with right sides together, pin, baste and sew frill to apron. Using seam binding, bind the frill seam to make neat.

QUICK MAKE

# Pretty party apron

A full-length, frilled, Edwardian-look apron to wear over a long skirt. Wear it just for fashion, or to keep you looking pretty as you dash between your guests and the kitchen.

**You will need:**
- ☐ Graph paper with 1 inch squares
- ☐ 2½ yards 36 inch wide cotton fabric
- ☐ Matching thread
- ☐ 1 yard ¾ inch wide matching seam binding

### The pattern

Using the graph paper, draw up the apron front and pocket pattern pieces to scale. Each square in the diagram represents a 1 inch square. Seam allowances are included.

### Cutting out

Following the layout, cut one apron front and one pocket from the cotton fabric. Also cut: one strip (a) 36 inches by 2 inches for the waist casing; four strips (b) each 36 inches by 2 inches, for the ties; two pieces (c) each 36 inches by 10 inches for the frill.

Cutting on the bias, as shown, cut two

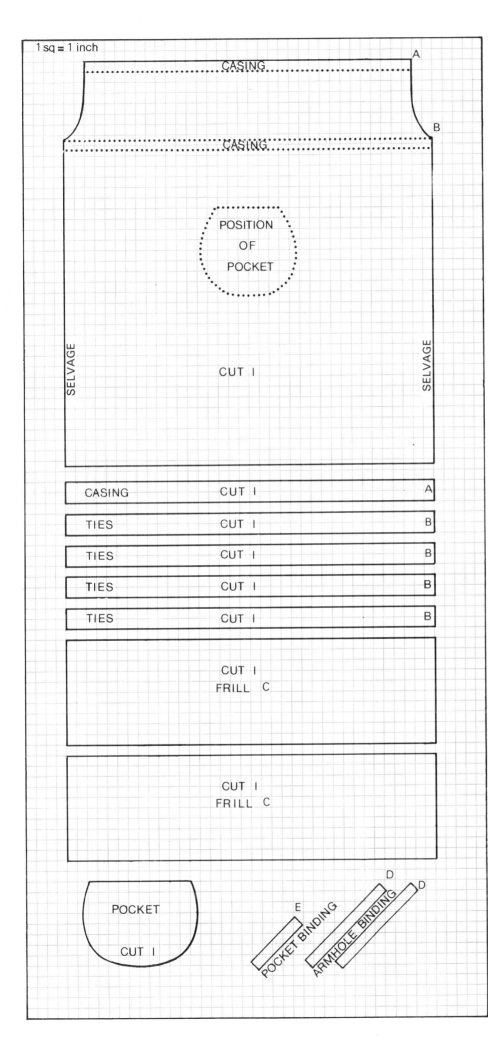

1 sq = 1 inch

CASING ·········· A

CASING ··········

CASING ·········· B

POSITION
OF
POCKET

SELVAGE

SELVAGE

CUT I

| CASING | CUT I | A |
| TIES | CUT I | B |
| TIES | CUT I | B |
| TIES | CUT I | B |
| TIES | CUT I | B |

CUT I
FRILL C

CUT I
FRILL C

POCKET

CUT I

E POCKET BINDING

D ARMHOLE BINDING D

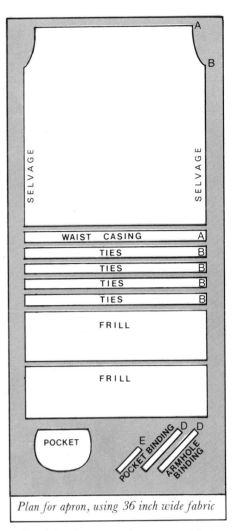

A

B

SELVAGE

SELVAGE

| WAIST CASING | A |
| TIES | B |
| TIES | B |
| TIES | B |
| TIES | B |

FRILL

FRILL

POCKET

E POCKET BINDING

D D ARMHOLE BINDING

*Plan for apron, using 36 inch wide fabric*

◄ *Graph for the apron – 1 square = 1 inch*

*The apron without the frill, with pockets*

# MACHINE KNITTING

# Easy-make kimono

Knitting by machine is a rapid process, so it is important to have the simplest possible directions which are easy to follow while working.

Creative Hands has evolved a new style of machine knitting pattern in which the finished shape of the garment is given as a working chart and the working directions are read alongside, from the cast-on edge upwards. The pattern has been worded especially to enable the kimono to be worked on any make of machine.

**To read the chart**
The chart gives the shape of the garment. The directions are alongside and are read in steps from the bottom paragraph first which is shown at the same level as the hem, then the next paragraph up etc.

## Kimono

### Size
Directions are for 32 to 38in bust.

---

### Gauge
8sts and 15 rows to 1 in.

---

### Materials
3-ply Fingering Yarn
About 4 oz.

### Finishing
**Braid (optional).** Using 2 or more strands together across 3 sts, set machine to work tubular knitting and make sufficient to go around front and neck edge and another length to go across bust line with ties.
Join side and underarm seams.
Stitch braid in position. Press.

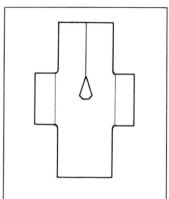

*Diagram showing the finished shape of the kimono*

---

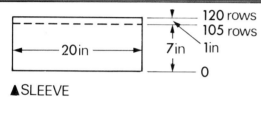

```
                          120 rows
                          105 rows
   ← 20in →      7in       1in
                          0
```
▲SLEEVE

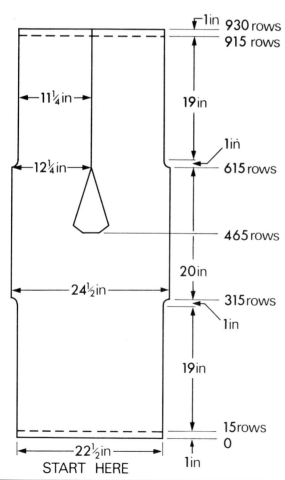

```
              ┌1in    930 rows
                      915 rows
  ←11¼in→       19in

  ←12¼in→       1in
                      615 rows

                      465 rows

              20in
  ←24½in→
                      315 rows
                      1in

              19in

                      15 rows
  ←22½in→      1in    0
  START HERE
```

**16.** Change to a loose gauge after row 105. Change back to main gauge after row 106. Knit straight to row 120. Bind off.

**15.** Knit straight to row 105.

**14.** Row counter to 0 and with WS facing, pick up 160 sts along sleeve edge.

**13.** Leaving cam box on the right side, put all needles into working position, turn the row counter back to 465 and complete the left side. Follow the directions from *.

**12.** Change to a loose gauge after row 915. Change back to main gauge after row 916. Knit straight to row 930. Bind off.

**11.** Work straight to row 915.

**10.** Dec one st at armhole edge after rows 615, 617, 619, 621, 623, 625, 627, 629.

**9.** At neck edge, inc one st after rows 486, 494, 502, 510, 518, 526, 534, 542, 550, 558, 566, 574, 582, 590, 598, 606, 614.

**8.** At neck edge, dec one st after rows 468, 470, 472, 474, 476, 478.

**7.** *On cam-box side, bind off 3 sts after row 467.

**6.** On cam-box side, bind off 16 sts after row 465.

**5.** Knit straight to row 465. Put 90 needles on left side into holding position and complete right side first.

**4.** On each side inc one st after rows 300, 302, 304, 306, 308, 310, 312, 314.

**3.** Knit straight to row 300.

**2.** Knit straight to row 14. Change to a loose gauge after row 14. Change back to main gauge after row 15.

**1.** Cast on 180 sts.

## START HERE

### Working with a different yarn

Should the garment be preferred in a thicker yarn, provided it is possible to achieve the same gauge, i.e. 8 stitches and 15 rows to the inch, the garment can be worked from the directions given.

Experiment with various gauges until you find the correct one to use, remembering to leave the knitted sample for 24 hours before taking a final measurement. To calculate the quantity of yarn required, knit up one ball of the chosen yarn at the correct gauge and count the number of stitches knitted (multiply the number of stitches by the number of rows).

The kimono has approximately 209,500 stitches. Divide this number by the number of stitches in the 1 oz swatch for the number of balls which will be required.

### Working at a different gauge

If you prefer to make the kimono in a substantially thicker yarn which cannot achieve the given gauge, work only from the measurements given on the chart.

Once the gauge is decided, it is a simple matter to know how many rows will be required or how many stitches to achieve the measurements given. For example, if the gauge is 6 stitches and 10 rows to the inch, there would be 135 cast-on stitches ($22\frac{1}{2}$ inches × 6) and 10 rows would make the 1 inch hem.

The yarn quantity is calculated by finding the number of stitches in 1 square inch at the gauge set and in the chosen yarn and dividing this number into 1723, which is the approximate number of square inches making up the completed kimono.

# The country mice take a stroll

When the cat's away . . . the mice take a walk in the woods. Mr. and Mrs. Mouse and their three children are a happy family to make from small pieces of felt and fabric scraps.

To make the whole family you will need:
- [ ] Scraps of red, navy, light green, green, white, pink and bright pink felt
- [ ] 1 12 inch square gray felt
- [ ] 1 12 inch square flesh-colored felt
- [ ] $\frac{1}{2}$ yard thin piping cord
- [ ] $\frac{1}{8}$ yard white and red pin dotted cotton fabric
- [ ] An assortment of tiny beads
- [ ] $\frac{1}{8}$ yard white and red polka dotted cotton fabric
- [ ] $\frac{1}{8}$ yard white and red striped cotton fabric
- [ ] $\frac{1}{2}$ yard 1 inch-deep black lampshade fringing
- [ ] Transparent sewing thread, for whiskers
- [ ] 1 package pipe cleaners
- [ ] D.M.C. 6-strand floss in light and deep pink
- [ ] Latex adhesive
- [ ] Kapok, for stuffing
- [ ] 1 thin (No. 2 or 3) steel knitting needle
- [ ] 2 12 inch squares thin cardboard

## Father mouse

Make a paper pattern from the graph. Note that for the larger mice, the scale is 1 square to one inch. Cut one large body from gray felt, two ears and one base. Cut two more ears from pink felt and two bases from cardboard, and a 7 inch length of piping cord, for tail. Fold the body piece in half and machine stitch down the side, with $\frac{1}{8}$ inch seam. Turn body to right side. Using stab-stitch sew the felt base to the body leaving half the base open. Stuff the body firmly with kapok, ramming it into the point of the nose with a pencil.
Insert the two cardboard bases trimming them a fraction smaller than the felt base. Tie a knot in one end of piping cord and insert this end into the base of mouse body; the knot prevents the tail from slipping out. Stitch up the rest of the base.

### To make the features

For the nose, work several satin stitches close together at the tip and over the seam using six strands of pale pink floss. For whiskers, stitch several short lengths of transparent sewing thread right through the head, just behind the nose, knotting them securely each side of the nose, to keep them in place. Trim whiskers to the desired length. For eyes, stitch a tiny bead to each side of the head. Using latex adhesive or fabric adhesive, stick a pink inner ear on one side of each of the two gray ears, pinch ears together at flat edge, and overcast. Then stitch ears to head, at an angle.

### To make the clothes

Cut one large collar from white felt, four hands from pink felt, one hat and one jacket from the green felt, including two sleeves, and one vest from the white and red polka dotted cotton fabric. Glue the vest to the mouse body, sewing some tiny beads to the front for buttons. Stick the coat over the vest. With the sharp knitting needle, pierce a hole right through body, where the arms are to go. Hold a pipe cleaner in line with the point of the needle and gradually withdraw the needle, pushing the pipe cleaner through the hole in body as you do so. Bend the ends of the pipe cleaner over, for hands. Fold the felt sleeves in half lengthwise and glue them over the pipe cleaner arms, with the joins underneath. Stick pink felt hands in position. The white collar goes on next around the top of the coat. Cut a very small oblong of navy felt, for a tie, round off the ends, and

▲ *The mouse family, two large mice and three small ones, brightly dressed in felt and fabric scraps*

stitch in place. Work around the middle of the bow with thread to achieve a bow effect. Gather a narrow length of red felt to make a flower, stitching a bead in the center. Make two tiny leaves and a stem in green felt and stitch to flower. Stitch flower to coat.

To make the hat, stitch the side seam of the hat piece and then sew on the crown and brim. Cut a narrow strip of red felt for a hatband, and glue it in place. Stitch the hat to the mouse's

hand and bend the arms into shape.

## Mother mouse

Make as for father mouse, using flesh-colored felt for body and outer ears, and bright pink felt for inner ears. The red and white polka-dotted skirt is a strip measuring 24 inches by $5\frac{3}{4}$ inches. To make it, stitch the center back seam, turn over $\frac{1}{4}$ inch at top and work two rows of tiny gathering stitches close to the top. Make a $\frac{1}{4}$ inch hem around

the bottom of the skirt. Gather up the top of the skirt to fit around the mouse body and stitch in place. Cut out the shawl from bright pink felt and sew black fringe all around the edge. Fold it as shown in the illustration and sew. Make a necklace from tiny beads.

## The small mice

The same method is used for making the small mice but note that the graph scale becomes $\frac{1}{2}$ inch to 1 square.

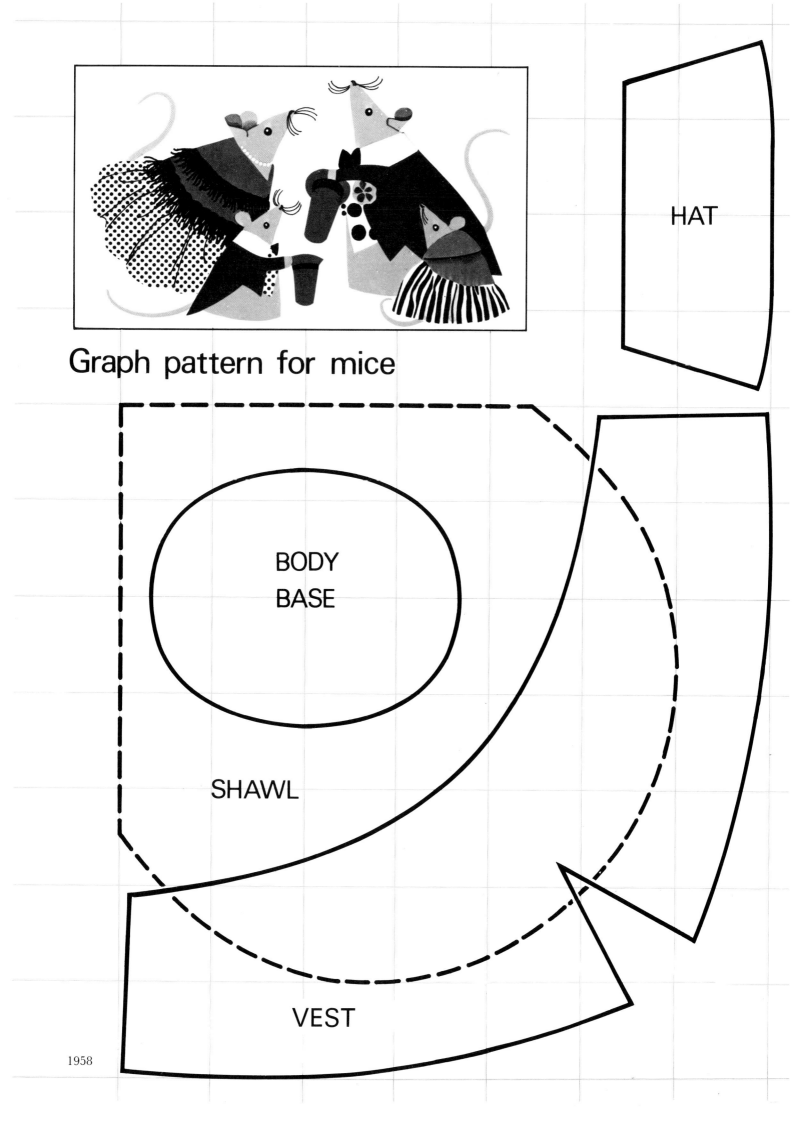

Graph pattern for mice

HAT

BODY
BASE

SHAWL

VEST

1958

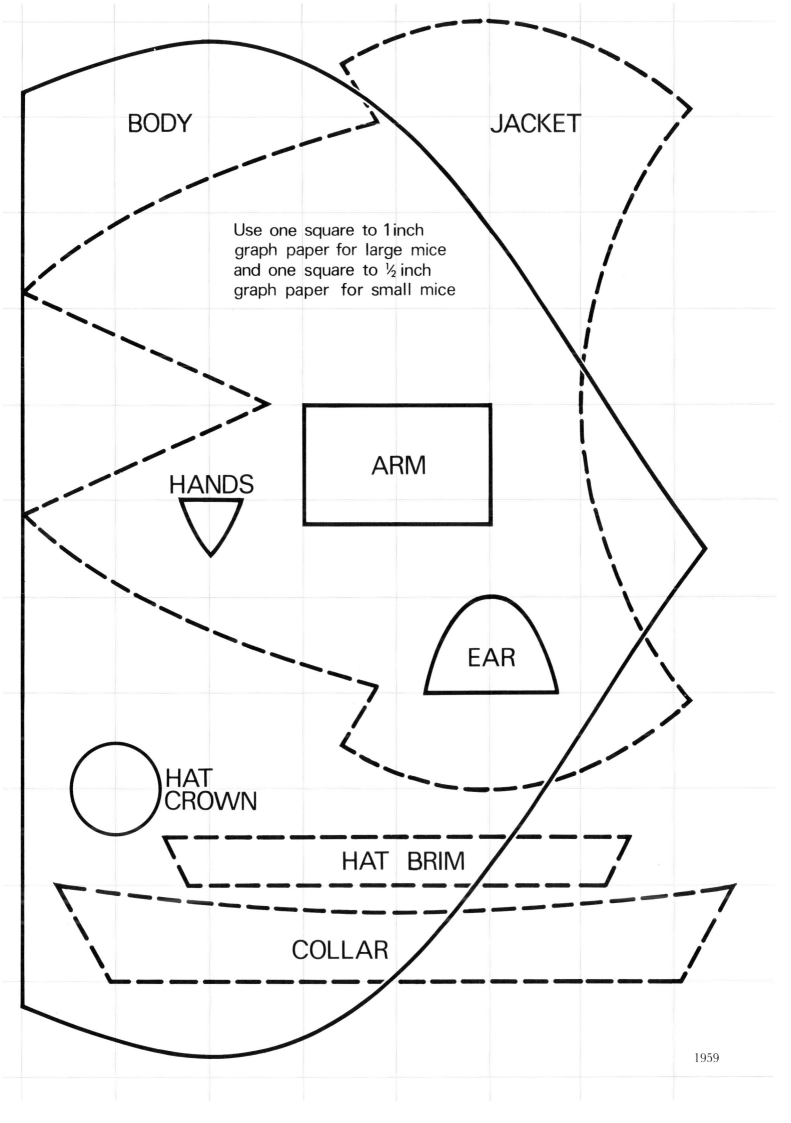

BODY

JACKET

Use one square to 1 inch
graph paper for large mice
and one square to ½ inch
graph paper for small mice

ARM

HANDS

EAR

HAT
CROWN

HAT BRIM

COLLAR

1959

*Beads and embroidery stitches combine with felt in vivid colors to transform simple butterfly designs into gay appliqué pillows*

# Fanciful felt

The decorative challenge of these felt appliqué pillows lies in choosing beads and embroidery stitches to embellish the felt butterfly shapes.

## To make the pillows

### Materials required to make each pillow measuring 13 inches square:

- [ ] two pieces of felt 14 inches square
- [ ] one piece of felt 11 inches square in a contrasting color
- [ ] one smaller scrap of felt in another contrasting color, for body
- [ ] one piece of tissue or tracing paper 12 inches square for making pattern
- [ ] 6-strand floss, pearl cotton or matte embroidery threads
- [ ] assorted beads and sequins
- [ ] sewing thread, cotton or silk
- [ ] beading needle (available in sizes 10 to 13)
- [ ] one pillow form 14 inches square
- [ ] one 12 inch zipper

### Transferring the design

The tracing pattern given here includes a different design on each wing. The body and antennae shapes are the same on each pillow. After tracing the body and antennae onto tissue or tracing paper, trace a pattern of the chosen wing on the same paper. One pattern piece can be used for both wings by drawing in the markings on one side with a felt pen, then turning it over and tracing them onto the reverse side. Pin the body and wing pattern pieces to the felt, then outline and transfer the markings using dressmaker's carbon paper. Turn over the wing pattern piece and repeat the process for the opposite wing. Cut out these shapes from the felt. No finishing off is required before stitching the pieces to the background felt.

### Basic stitches

The basic butterfly shapes are applied to a background surface of felt with either a straight machine stitch or zigzag stitch. The antennae are all worked in stem stitch and the decorative work on the wings is a combination of chain and stem stitch.

### To apply beads

Beads and sequins can be applied in straight lines or curves; often the most effective device is to group them in small areas, as on the bodies of the butterflies shown here. The tension of the stitches used for beading should be firm, but not too tight or the effect is spoiled.

### Making the pillows

Place the plain square of felt to the appliquéd piece, right sides facing. Baste and machine stitch around the sides, taking $\frac{1}{2}$ inch seam allowance and leaving a 12 inch opening along one side for inserting the zipper. Turn to the right side. Pin, baste and machine stitch zipper into place. Insert pillow form.

QUICK MAKE
# Caftans-long or short

1962

This elegant caftan is quick and simple to make. Wear it full length as a dinner dress or a more casual house robe, or cut it short for a pretty top to wear over pants or a long skirt.

## Measurements

The pattern and instructions given here are to fit a $32\frac{1}{2}$ inch to 38 inch bust size. The back neck to hem measurement for the long version is $59\frac{1}{2}$ inches and for the short version $26\frac{1}{2}$ inches.

Add a 1 inch seam allowance down the center front and all side edges and a 1 inch hem. On all other edges allow $\frac{1}{2}$ inch.

It is advisable to wash or pre-shrink both fabric and lace before cutting out.

## Requirements

### For long version
☐ $2\frac{1}{4}$ yards 54 inch wide wool fabric or 4 yards of 36 inch wide cotton fabric

### For short version
☐ $2\frac{1}{4}$ yards 36 inch wide cotton fabric

### For both versions
☐ 1 yard 3 inch wide lace
☐ $\frac{1}{8}$ yard of iron-on interfacing
☐ $\frac{1}{4}$ yard contrasting fabric
☐ matching mercerized sewing thread
☐ link button fastening (optional)

## Making the caftan

**1.** Mark the front darts with lines of basting stitches. Cut the length of lace in half and lay the pieces onto the fronts, overlapping the upper dart line. Baste in position then, using a small back-stitch, hand-stitch down both sides of each piece of lace.

**2.** With the right sides together stitch the front darts, thus anchoring the lower edges of the lace. Press the darts downward.

**3.** With right sides together, stitch the center front seam starting 7 inches from the neckline. Press seam open, then turn under and press the raw edges to make neat. Top-stitch down both sides of the center front seam from neck to hem.

**4.** With right sides together, stitch the shoulder seams. Press the seam toward the back. Turn work to right side and make two rows of top stitching, the first row $\frac{1}{16}$ inch from the seam and the second row $\frac{1}{8}$ inch away from the first row. Overcast the raw edges to make neat.

**5.** With right sides together, stitch the side seams from underarm to 21 inches from the bottom. (The short version is seamed right down to the hem.) Press and baste back the 1 inch seam allowances and make neat the raw edges by turning back $\frac{1}{8}$ inch and top-stitching. (For fine woolens and heavier fabrics,

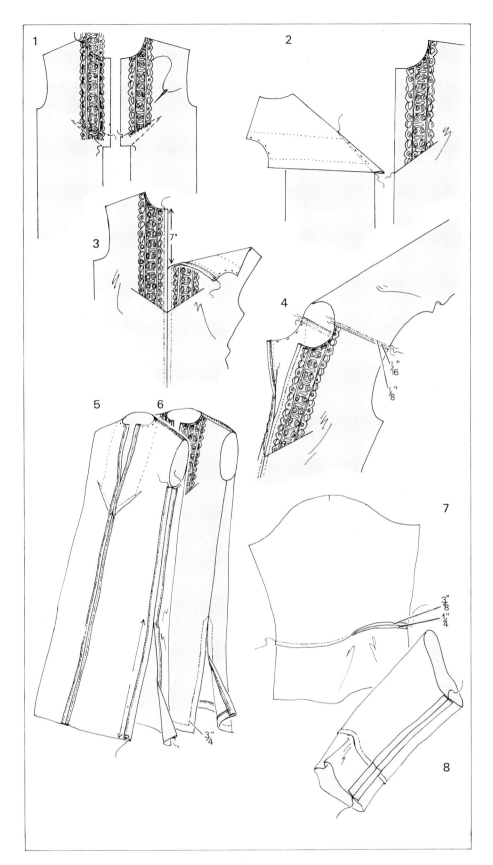

overcast the edges to make neat.)

**6.** Make neat the raw edges of the hem by overcasting. Turn up a 1 inch hem and baste. Top-stitch $\frac{3}{4}$ inch from the edge around the hem and the side slits.

**7.** With right sides together, stitch the cuffs to the sleeves. Trim the turnings to $\frac{1}{4}$ inch for the cuff and $\frac{3}{8}$ inch for the sleeve, then press both edges down-

ward away from the armhole edge.

**8.** With right sides together and the cuff seams matching, stitch the underarm seams. Press seams open.

**9.** Turn in and press $\frac{1}{2}$ inch seam allowance to the wrong side of the cuff, then fold cuff up and match the underarm seams. Stitch by hand to the previous line of machine stitching. Press cuff edge.

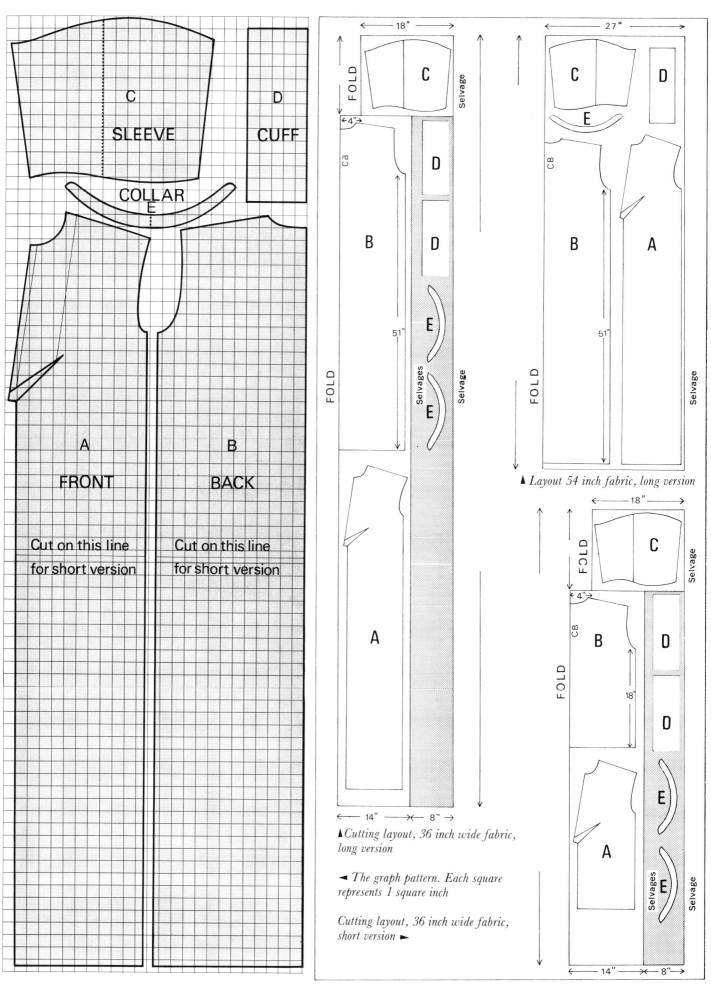

C
SLEEVE

D
CUFF

COLLAR
E

A
FRONT

Cut on this line
for short version

B
BACK

Cut on this line
for short version

1964

18"
FOLD
C
4"
CB
B
51"
A

D
D
E
E
Selvages
Selvage

← 14" → ← 8" →

▲ *Cutting layout, 36 inch wide fabric, long version*

◄ *The graph pattern. Each square represents 1 square inch*

*Cutting layout, 36 inch wide fabric, short version* ►

27"
C
D
E
CB
B
A
51"
FOLD
Selvage

▲ *Layout 54 inch fabric, long version*

18"
FOLD
C
4"
CB
B
18"
D
D
A
E
Selvages
E
Selvage

← 14" → ← 8" →

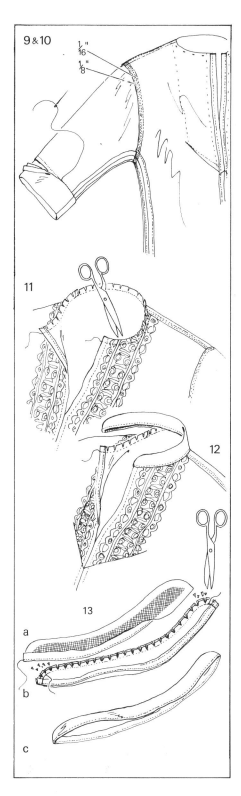

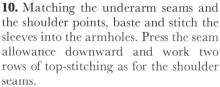

**10.** Matching the underarm seams and the shoulder points, baste and stitch the sleeves into the armholes. Press the seam allowance downward and work two rows of top-stitching as for the shoulder seams.

**11.** Using long machine stitches, sew around the neckline ½ inch from the edge. Clip all around, almost to the stitches.

**12.** Drop the collar band into place along the line of stitching, sandwiching the clipped edge. Baste and machine top-stitch.

**13.** If desired, close neck with a linked button fastening.

### To make a collar band
Cut the collar band and facing with ½ inch seam allowances. Cut the iron-on interfacing without turnings. The collar band can be made in matching or contrasting fabric.

**13a.** Position the interfacing centrally on the wrong side of the band and iron in place. Press up and top-stitch the lower edge of the seam allowance.

**b.** With right sides together, lay the band and facing together and stitch all around the top edge. Fasten off the thread securely at both ends. Layer and clip the seam allowance.

**c.** Turn band to right side. Turn up the seam allowance of the facing and press. Drop the collar band into place along the line of stitching, sandwiching the clipped edge and baste in position.

When stitching the collar band to the neckline, top-stitch entire edge.

# Putting the edge on it

A deep macramé fringe transforms a simple shawl into something really special. The shawl is shaped so that it will not slide off the shoulders, and takes only one yard of 36 inch wide fabric.

## Size

Center back 20in, excluding fringe
Center back neck to lower front edge
17½in, excluding fringe
Fringe 7½in

## Materials

Brown paper 17in by 30in
1yd 36in wide fabric
1yd 36in wide lining fabric
Tubular rayon cord: 3 100yd spools
350 5mm wooden beads
31 12mm wooden beads

## Shawl

Cut a rectangle of brown paper 17 inches by 30 inches and lay it on a flat surface with the 17 inch edges at the top and bottom. Mark the left edge 20½ inches up from the bottom corner and the right edge 11 inches up from the bottom corner.

Draw a pencil line from the left edge marking to the top right-hand corner (A–B), and from the right edge marking to the bottom left corner (C–D), thus forming a slanting diamond shape. Mark A–C as fold line, then cut along A–B and C–D. Measure and mark one inch down each line from point B, join the two points and cut along the line.

Fold fabric into a triangle and lay the fold line of the paper pattern to the fold line of the fabric. Pin the pattern in place. Cut one piece of main fabric and one lining.

Place fabric and lining wrong sides together and stitch all around, taking a ¼ inch seam allowance and leaving a 6 inch opening on the A–B edge. Turn right sides out through this opening, then slip stitch open edges together. Baste all around edges through both thicknesses and press.

## Macramé edging

Cut 345 threads each 30 inches long. This can be done quickly by winding the cord around a piece of stiff cardboard 30 inches long. Tie the threads on each side of the cardboard with separate lengths of cord and cut the cords at each end of the cardboard.

Each scallop has 11 doubled threads set over a width of 2¼ inches with ⅛ inch space between the scallops. Thread each length into a chenille needle and insert it through the fabric about ⅛ inch from

the edge. Remove the needle and adjust the ends of the cord so that they are even before tying an overhand knot close to the fabric edge.

Begin at center point C. Set one thread on the exact point, then five threads evenly each side of the center thread to form the first scallop.

## Scallop

Using outside threads as leaders, cord diagonally into the center over eleven threads. Pass both leaders through the center of a large bead.

Counting from the outer edges in, put a small bead on every second thread. Using outside threads as leaders, cord diagonally over nine threads.

Using outside threads as leaders, work a second row of cording over nine threads. Work an overhand knot with the four center threads immediately under the large bead.

## Positioning the scallops

Work seven scallops on each side of the central one.

At the D corners, set on one thread at the point of the corner with six threads on each side of it, thus working the scallop over thirteen threads with six small beads on each side, to weight these corners.

Continue from D to B on both sides of the shawl, working six more complete scallops and ending with the seventh and final scallop set with six threads on the remaining part of the straight edge D–B, and five threads set on the one inch cut-off corners (marked on the diagram as B–E).

## Trimming the fringe

Measure 5 inches from the bottom of the overhand knot under each big bead and trim all along fringe.

Remove basting threads.

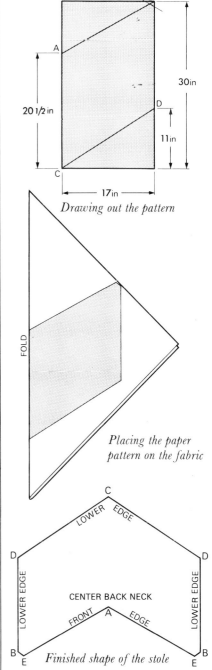

*Drawing out the pattern*

*Placing the paper pattern on the fabric*

*Finished shape of the stole*

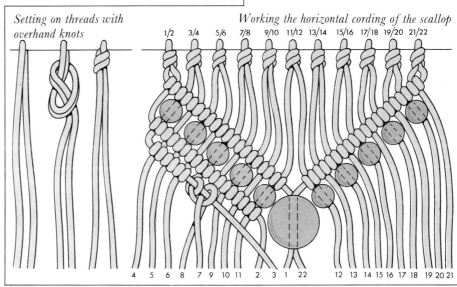

*Setting on threads with overhand knots*

*Working the horizontal cording of the scallop*

1968

# Noah's Ark

Mr. and Mrs. Noah and the animals pose for a group photograph before trooping into the Ark. Made from felt and polyurethane foam, these charming toys show a wealth of detail and imagination. Instructions are given for making the cardboard Ark, too.

Basic materials needed for making Mr. and Mrs. Noah and the animals are given below. Materials needed to cover and decorate each item are given under specific instructions.

### You will need:
☐ Two large sheets of stiff paper, for patterns
☐ Two 18 inch squares of 1 inch deep polyurethane foam
☐ Black felt-tip pen
☐ Latex adhesive
☐ Xacto knife or a small hacksaw or fretsaw, to cut polyurethane

## Mr. and Mrs. Noah

### You will need:
☐ Materials given in general instructions
☐ One 12 inch square maroon felt
☐ One 5 inch by 3 inch piece peach felt
☐ One 5 inch square orange felt
☐ One $5\frac{1}{4}$ inch square black felt
☐ One 5 inch by 3 inch piece light brown felt
☐ One 6 inch by 5 inch piece yellow-green felt
☐ 1 oz thin gold twine or knitting yarn, for Noah's crook
☐ One 4 inch square white felt
☐ Scraps of dark green, yellow, pink and mauve felt, and gold and pearl beads, for trimming
☐ 1 oz thick white knitting yarn
☐ 1 oz thick gold knitting yarn

### To make Mr. Noah
**Body:** Cut two blocks of 1 inch deep polyurethane, each 5 inches by 2 inches, and stick them together with the adhesive. For the body covering, cut strips of felt, each 5 inches long, as follows: one $\frac{1}{2}$ inch wide strip in maroon, one 1 inch wide strip in peach, one $1\frac{1}{4}$ inch strip in orange and one $2\frac{1}{4}$ inch wide strip in

▲ *Mr and Mrs Noah*  ▼ *The cats*  ▲ *The giraffes*  ▼ *The penguins and the fish*

maroon. Stitch the long sides of the strips together, in the order given, to make a 5 inch square.

**To cover the body:** Wrap the joined strips of felt around the joined foam blocks, wrong side to the polyurethane foam, with the narrow maroon strip at the top. Overcast the edges of the felt together so that the join is in the center of one of the larger sides of the foam shape, stripes running horizontally.

**Top of hat:** Cut a $1\frac{1}{2}$ inch diameter circle from maroon felt and sew it to the top of Noah's head. Using matching thread, run a gathering thread around the lower edge of the side of the hat crown, and draw it up slightly.

**Hat brim:** Cut a $2\frac{3}{4}$ inch diameter circle of thick cardboard and pierce a $1\frac{1}{2}$ inch diameter circle in the center, without cutting into the outer circle. Cut two brim shapes from maroon felt and sew it to the inch diameter circle from the center, without cutting into the outer

circle. Cut two brim shapes from maroon felt, making each a fraction larger than the cardboard, and overcast them together with the cardboard in the middle. Push the brim down into position over the maroon felt crown, and catch-stitch firmly in place.

**Arms:** For each arm, cut a 5 inch length of pipe cleaner and fold it in half. Cut a 1 inch by $\frac{3}{4}$ inch piece of peach felt for each hand and fold it in half lengthwise. Glue each hand over the folded ends of the pipe cleaners, rounding off one corner.

**Sleeves:** Cut two pieces, each $1\frac{3}{4}$ inches by $1\frac{1}{2}$ inches, from the orange felt. Fold each in half lengthwise, place one over each arm and stitch in place, so the hands are overlapped a little. Round off each sleeve head. Using matching thread, stitch the arms to Noah's sides, just below the join of the orange and peach felt.

**Hair, beard and features:** The hair

and beard are loops of thick white knitting yarn, couched down lightly. All the features are made from felt. Mark the legs in black yarn.

**Dove and trimmings:** Using the same-size shape given here, cut two dove shapes in white felt, adding a fringed tail. Pad the dove with a little absorbent cotton, add a yellow felt beak and embroider the wing and eye in black thread. Cut a green felt olive branch, glue it in the dove's beak, and stitch the dove to Noah's right hand. Trim Noah's front with two gold buttons, and make a crook shape with two pipe cleaners twisted together. Bind around the entire crook with gold twine and stitch it to Noah's left hand.

**To make base:** Cut a $2\frac{1}{2}$ inch diameter cardboard circle and cover the sides with slightly larger circles of black felt. Overcast felt circles together. Glue and carefully stitch the black disk to the base of the figure.

▲ *The horses*　　　　▼ *The swans*

▲ *The dogs*　　　　▼ *The snakes*

## To make Mrs. Noah

Cut two blocks of foam the same size as those used for Mr. Noah, and stick them together. For the body, cut strips of felt, each 5 inches long, as follows: one ½ inch wide strip in light brown, one 1 inch wide strip in peach, one 3½ inch wide strip in yellow-green. Stitch the long sides of the strips together to make a 5 inch square.

**To cover body:** Wrap the felt around the foam with light brown felt to the top, and attach as for Mr. Noah. For the hat crown, cut a 1½ inch diameter circle in light brown and sew it to the top of Mrs. Noah's head. Make a hat brim as described for Mr. Noah, using light brown felt. Make Mrs. Noah's arms as for Mr. Noah, using peach and yellow-green felt, and stitch to her body.

For dress, frill, cut a strip of yellow-green felt, ½ inch wide and 9 inches long. Join the short ends, gather one long edge, slip over the base of Mrs.

Noah's body, and overcast in place. The features are either made from glued-on felt or embroidered.

**Hair:** Glue loops of thick gold knitting yarn to sides and back of head, stitching with matching thread. Pull loops to the center back of head and coil a separate strand of yarn around, to suggest a bun, stitching it to center back of head.

**Trimming hat:** Make a dove as for Noah, but add a separate wing shape in white felt, to one side. Stitch the dove to the center front of Mrs. Noah's hat, and surround it with tiny felt flowers.

**To trim body:** Trim Mrs. Noah's body with small pearl buttons, whittle two matchsticks to points, for knitting needles, and add thick blue yarn to represent knitting. Stitch the knitting in place in Mrs. Noah's hands, as shown. Make a disk to glue to base of figure as described for Mr. Noah, using cardboard and light brown felt.

## Making the animals

### You will need:

☐ 12 inch squares of felt in the following colors: pale orange, mid brown, black, white, mauve, lavender, pale pink, navy, maroon, peach, bright orange, blue, yellow, green, mustard, pale yellow, cream, russet brown, beige, dark brown, ginger, emerald green, deep pink
☐ One piece black felt, 18 inches long by ½ inch wide, for giraffes' manes
☐ 1 oz thick navy knitting yarn, for horses' manes
☐ 1 oz thick white knitting yarn, for swans
☐ 6-strand embroidery floss, in the following colors: mid brown, black, white, turquoise, pink
☐ Two packets pipe cleaners
☐ Small beads, sequins, gold braid etc., for trimmings
☐ Matching sewing threads

# Tracing patterns for the animals

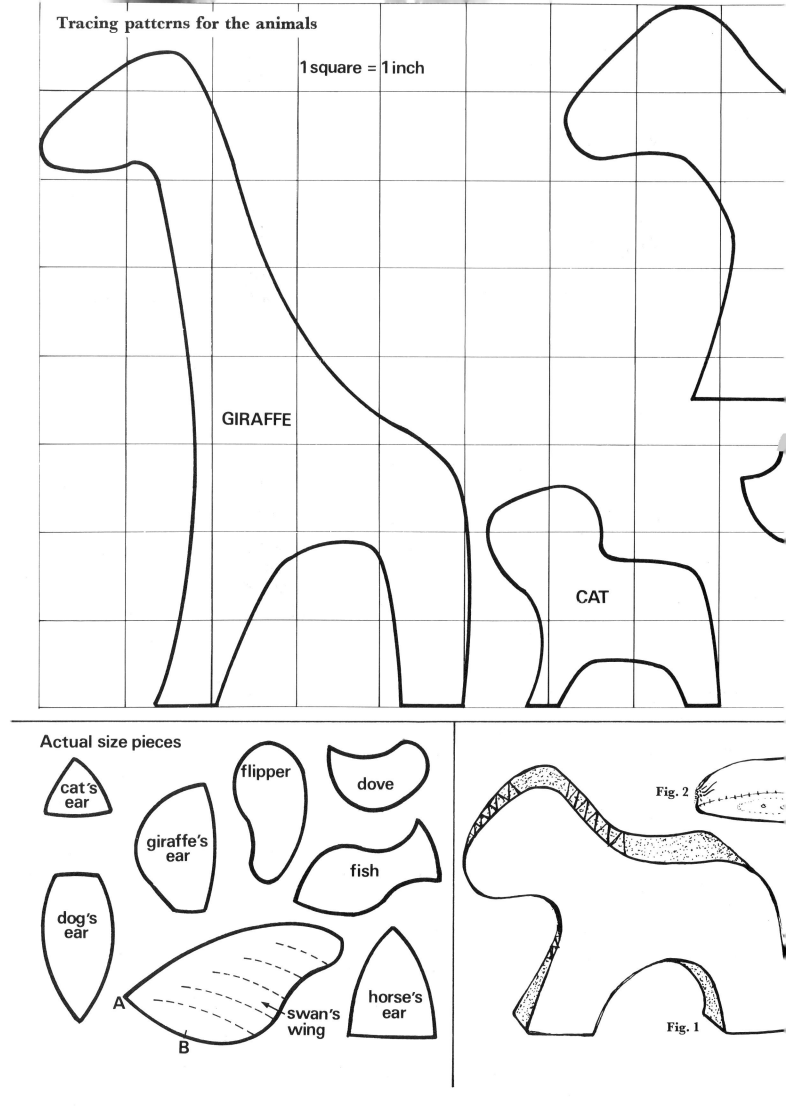

1 square = 1 inch

GIRAFFE

CAT

## Actual size pieces

cat's ear

giraffe's ear

flipper

dove

fish

dog's ear

A

B

swan's wing

horse's ear

Fig. 2

Fig. 1

1972

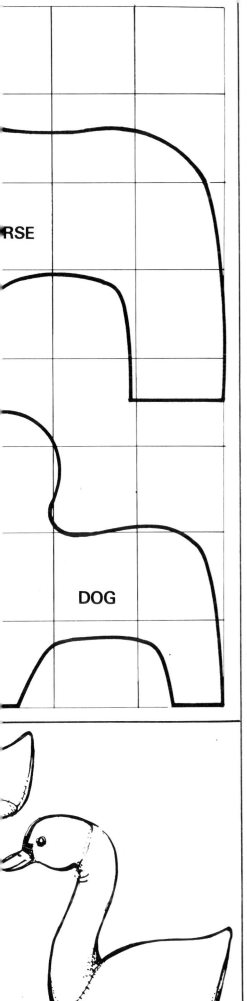

**RSE**

**DOG**

**Fig. 3**

☐ Absorbent cotton
☐ A large darning needle
☐ Two small dress weights

### The patterns

Working from the graph, in which one square represents 1 inch, make one stiff paper pattern for the giraffe, the cat, the dog and the horse. The other animals are made without complete body patterns, but have various parts added. These pattern pieces are shown same-size on the chart, and can be traced off directly.

### Cutting shapes from the foam

Place the paper pattern on the foam and, holding it steady, draw all around the shape with the felt-tip pen. Where possible, put the base of the leg shapes against the straight edge of the foam, so that the animals have a completely flat base to stand up on.

Cut two foam shapes for the giraffes and the horses, glueing them together with latex adhesive for extra thickness. The other animals are made from one thickness of foam.

Having drawn the shape of an animal on the foam, cut the straight edges of the shape with scissors; rounded edges are cut by holding the hacksaw or Xacto knife upright and working around each outline with an up-and-down sawing motion. Keep the blade at right angles to the sheet of foam.

### The basic method for making and shaping animals

Most of the animals are made in this way. To cover the sides of a foam shape, dab latex or similar adhesive lightly on one side of the shape and press it down onto the felt. Trim the felt to the edge of the foam and repeat with the other side of the shape.

### To shape animals

Before positioning gussets, shape animals by catching the edges of both felt side pieces together across the foam, with matching thread (figure 1). Shape necks and noses in this way.

**Gussets:** Measure around the foam outline of each animal to find the gusset length. Cut a strip of felt this length, making it $1\frac{3}{4}$ inches wide for the double thickness animals, $\frac{7}{8}$ inch wide for the single thickness animals. Stitch pieces of felt together to make up the length if necessary.

**To attach the gussets:** Dab adhesive lightly along the center of the uncovered foam edges and stick the gusset into place right around the animal outline, so that the join or joins come under the body or feet of the animals. Stab the

gusset at intervals with pins, to hold it while the adhesive dries. There will be overhanging edges of felt in the areas where the foam has been compressed, trim away the surplus to fit.

Using matching thread, neatly overcast both edges of the gusset to the edges of the side pieces, then overcast the short ends of the gusset strip together where they meet.

### Giraffes

Using pale orange felt for the bodies and two thicknesses of foam for each animal, make up two giraffes, using the basic method described. Shape and compress the necks at front and back, to make them more slender.

Make **the manes** from strips of black felt, about 18 inches long by $\frac{1}{4}$ inch wide, sewing the strips in spirals down each giraffe's neck from forehead, extending down the back of the neck for about 4 inches. Make **the hooves** from black felt, as shown in picture, and indicate the legs by couching down double strands of black 6-strand embroidery floss.

Make **the tails** from strips of orange felt stitched around with loops of black stranded floss. For horns, cut a $2\frac{1}{2}$ inch long piece of pipe cleaner. Cut small slits on each side of each giraffe's forehead and push the pipe cleaner through the slits. Bend up the ends as shown and cover with small circles of mid brown felt. Using the same size shape given, cut four ears from pale orange felt and stitch to giraffes' heads. Make **the eyes** as shown in the detail picture, padding the female giraffes' eyelids with a little absorbent cotton. Make the features as shown in the picture.

### Horses

Make the horses from two thicknesses of foam each, using the felts and other materials shown in the picture and shaping at necks and noses.

### Dogs

Make the dogs from one thickness only of the foam, using the felts and other materials shown in the picture, shaping necks and noses. If the dogs will not stand securely, cover a small piece of cardboard with matching felt and attach to base of each leg.

### Cats

Make two cats from one thickness only of the foam, using the felts and other materials shown in the picture, shaping necks and noses and inserting a 1 inch length of $\frac{7}{8}$ inch wide cream felt in the gussets, for fronts. Stitch this part between front and back legs.

**Penguins**
For each penguin, cut a 2 inch by $1\frac{3}{4}$ inch piece of 1 inch thick foam. For each body, cut a piece of white felt, $3\frac{1}{2}$ inches by $2\frac{1}{4}$ inches; wrap the felt around the foam and overcast the shorter edges together. Gather one edge of the felt and stitch the gathers (this becomes the top of the head). Repeat. Cut a $3\frac{1}{2}$ inch by $2\frac{1}{2}$ inch rectangle of black felt for each penguin. Join the short edges together for $\frac{3}{4}$ inch at one end and run a gathering thread around the joined long edge, to make a "wigwam" shape.
Pull the black felt shape over the white body and sew lower long edge of black shape to lower edge of white felt, leaving a triangular piece of white felt showing for penguin's front. Repeat. Make beaks, feet and eyes, as shown in picture.
**Bases:** For each penguin cut a $1\frac{1}{2}$ inch diameter circle of black felt. Trim where necessary and stitch to base of each bird.
**Wings:** Cut four white wings and four black wings, from felt. Sew together in pairs and stitch two wings to each penguin, as shown in picture.
**Fishes:** Using the same size shape given, cut four shapes in yellow felt. Stitch together, padding lightly with cotton and add eyes and mouths as shown. Embroider straight tail markings and buttonhole stitch scales in orange floss. Glue a fish under each penguin's left wing.

**Swans**
Cut two ovals of 1 inch thick plastic foam, 2 inches long by $1\frac{1}{4}$ inches wide and two rectangles of white felt, $2\frac{3}{4}$ inches by $2\frac{1}{2}$ inches. Taper each short side of one felt piece so one long side measures $1\frac{1}{4}$ inches. Fold the felt in half lengthwise so tapering sides are together, and stitch up the longer short side. This is the tail end. Turn the felt so the join is on the inside and gather up the shorter end as much as possible. Repeat.
**Bases:** Cut four ovals in white felt, the same size as the foam ovals, and sew together in pairs, inserting a small dress weight in each. Glue the felt ovals to the foam ovals. Pin the shaped upper body pieces to the uncovered side of the foam bases, with the tail ends centered at one end of each oval. Overcast the edges of bases and upper bodies together (figure 2).
**Necks:** Cut four $3\frac{1}{2}$ inch lengths of pipe cleaner and twist two together. Cut a $\frac{1}{2}$ inch square of orange felt and glue and stitch to cover one end of the pipe cleaners, for beak. Cut a $3\frac{1}{4}$ inch by $1\frac{1}{4}$ inch piece of white felt, for the rest of the neck. Wind thick white knitting yarn closely around the uncovered portion of the pipe cleaners, to pad the neck, then fold the felt in half lengthwise around it. Using matching thread, overcast the edges of the felt together, padding where necessary with tiny pieces of cotton. Repeat.
**Heads:** Cut two pieces of $1\frac{3}{4}$ inch by $\frac{1}{2}$ inch white felt; stitch short ends together. Slip this small tube over necks of swans, just above the beaks, and run a gathering thread through each free edge. Insert a little cotton to round out the heads, draw up the gathering threads, and overcast heads to necks. Mark nostrils and beaks as shown, and stitch tiny black beads to each head, for eyes (figure 3).
**Joining necks to bodies:** Place the lower end of the neck to the gathered front of the body and, with the end of the neck even with the base, stitch neck in place, drawing the felt of the body around the base of the neck. Bend neck into a curve. Repeat.
**Wings:** Using the same-size shape shown here, cut eight wings in white felt. Overcast together in pairs along the upper edge, from A to the tip. Cut 2 inches of pipe cleaner for each double wing and apply a little adhesive to the pipe cleaners; stick the pipe cleaners between the felt wings, along each curve, bending them to follow the curves. Pad the rest of each wing with a little cotton and overcast the wings, to close. Work lines of running stitch in white thread through all thicknesses, as indicated, to suggest feathers. Overcast wings from A to B, to the base of each swan, as shown in picture.

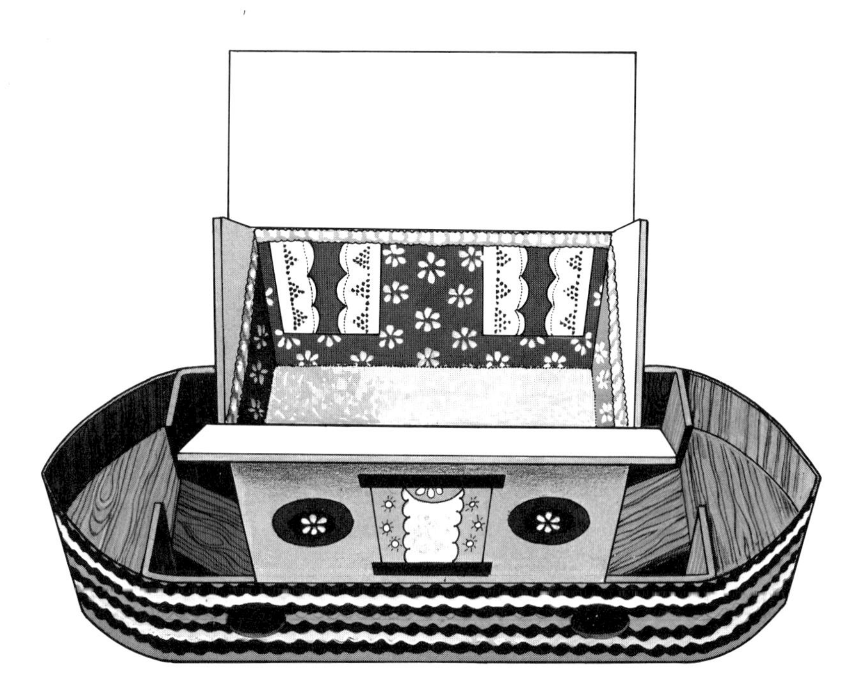
*The completed Ark with the top open*

**Snakes**
Each snake consists of four pipe cleaners twisted together and bound with thick knitting yarn until the felt covering fits snugly.
**Body coverings:** Cut four strips of felt, each $6\frac{3}{4}$ inches by $\frac{5}{8}$ inch, two in bright pink, one in mauve and one in emerald green. Overcast one long edge of the mauve strip and one bright pink strip, to join, and repeat with other strips. Wrap one joined strip around one snake body and overcast to join, adding cotton padding if necessary. Gather the short edges of the strip and overcast. Repeat.
**Heads:** For each head, cut two felt pieces, each 1 inch square, from the body colors. Overcast two sides of one pair of felt pieces, put the tube over one end of the snake, gather, and pad, matching the colors to the body. Repeat. Decorate as shown in picture, placing sequins or fancy braid down the back of the snakes.
**Features:** Make eyes as shown. Embroider mouths on each snake as shown, then cut a $1\frac{1}{4}$ inch length of thin brass wire for each tongue. Twist tiny black beads on the ends of the wire and fold the wire in half. Poke a tiny hole in snake's head, just above the center of the mouth, insert the folded end of the wire and stitch securely in place. Repeat.

## Ark

**You will need:**
- ☐ One cardboard box (the one illustrated measures $13\frac{1}{2}$ inches by 7 inches, $4\frac{1}{4}$ inches deep)

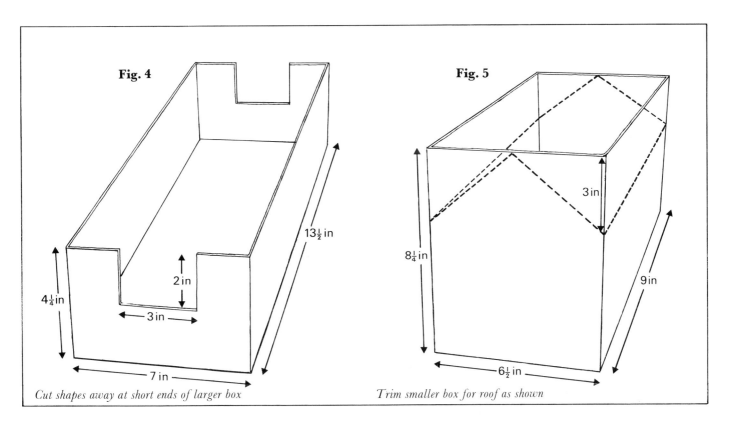

Fig. 4

13½ in

2 in

4¼ in

3 in

7 in

*Cut shapes away at short ends of larger box*

Fig. 5

3 in

8¼ in

9 in

6½ in

*Trim smaller box for roof as shown*

☐ Two 9½ inch by 4 inch pieces of card-
board
☐ Masking tape
☐ Two 6½ inch by 3¼ inch pieces of
cardboard
☐ Two 3½ inch by 3 inch pieces of card-
board
☐ Small hacksaw or Xacto knife
☐ Scraps of wood-patterned wallpaper
☐ Wallpaper paste
☐ One cardboard box (the one illus-
trated measures 9 inches by 6½ inches,
8¼ inches deep)
☐ Two 24 inch square sheets white
paper
☐ Adhesive or white glue
☐ 6 inch squares of yellow, purple and
pink felt
☐ Two 9½ inch by 4½ inch pieces of
cardboard
☐ Two 9¾ inch by 5¼ inch pieces of red
bonded jersey fabric, for roof
☐ Pinking shears
☐ ¼ yard 36 inch wide printed cotton
fabric, for lining cabin
☐ Scraps of braid to trim cabin
☐ Scraps of 1¼ inch deep eyelet embroidery, for window trimmings
☐ Piece of printed synthetic jersey
fabric, 47 inches by 5 inches, to cover
boat
☐ Scrap of synthetic fur fabric, to cover
cabin floor

The following directions are for a Noah's
Ark with finished measurements 27
inches by 13 inches.
**Making the Ark**
**To make the boat shape:** Cut a 3 inch

by 2 inch piece from both short ends of
the larger box (see figure 4).
Bend the two 9½ inch by 4 inch pieces
of cardboard in half, gently, and attach
them to the short ends of the larger box
with masking tape, so they represent
bows and stern.
**To make decks and gangways:**
Trim the two 6½ inch by 3¼ inch pieces
of cardboard so they fit inside bows and
stern and attach them inside each end
with masking tape, 2 inches down from
the top, so they are in line with the openings cut in the box.
Attach the 3½ inch by 3 inch pieces of
cardboard with masking tape to the two
decks thus made, and the base of the
boat, so they form sloping gangways.
**Portholes:** Cut 1¾ inch diameter portholes in the long sides of the box, using
the Xacto knife and starting the outside porthole 1¼ inches in from the
corners.
**To finish:** Cover the sides and floors
of the two decks and gangways and the
upper side of the boat base with wood-
patterned wallpaper.
**To make cabin windows:** Cut windows in the long sides of the smaller
cardboard box, making each 2½ inches
by 2 inches; center one window and cut
two windows on either side of it, positioning them so each is ½ inch from the
box corners.
**To join cabin to boat:** Center the
cabin on the boat shape and attach it
with masking tape. Cover the four sides
of the smaller box in white paper, using
wallpaper paste to attach it and running

the paper down over the boat shape,
to strengthen the join. Cut X-shapes over
each window, push the paper to the
inside, and paste down.
**To trim:** Make a felt front door and
trim the windows with decorative scraps
of felt in various colors, as shown in the
picture.
**The roof:** Cover one side of each of the
two pieces of 9½ inch by 4½ inch card
with the pieces of red bonded jersey, for
roof, glueing the jersey in position. Trim
lower edges of jersey with pinking shears.
Cutting 3 inches down from the top,
trim the smaller box, as shown in figure
5, to make the roof shape. Attach the
pieces of jersey-covered cardboard to the
top of each long side of the cabin with
masking tape. This makes the roof,
which can be opened. A shoelace in a
bright color can be threaded through
each side of the roof, so the ark can be
opened up and fastened again as required.
**Trimming the inside of the cabin:**
Cover the cabin interior with the printed
cotton fabric, turning in the raw edges
and glueing. Trim all around the top of
the interior with a length of braid. Glue
scraps of eyelet embroidery inside each
window as shown, for curtains.
**To complete:** Cover the boat shape
with the long piece of jersey fabric. Turn
in the raw edges and glue, positioning
the fabric so the join comes at bows or
stern, glueing particularly thoroughly
around the portholes. When adhesive is
dry, carefully cut out portholes through
the fabric with the craft knife.

# Soft touch

This tiny, soft mohair top is another of our special designs for machine knitting. You can work it from our easy-to-follow directions on any make of knitting machine.

**Sizes**

Directions are for 32in bust. The figures in brackets [] refer to the 34 and 36in bust sizes respectively.

**Materials**

Reynolds Wendy Whisper
7 [8:9] 25 grm. balls
One No. E (3.50 mm)
crochet hook
2¾ [3:3] yds. purchased braid

**Finishing**

With RS facing, pin out to measurements. Steam, using a steam iron held one inch from the surface of the garment. Leave until completely dry.

**Edging.** Join armband seams. Work edging along both edges of armbands and along top edge of front and back pieces.

**1st row** Using No. E hook, work 1 row sc. Turn.

**2nd row** Ss to 2nd sc, 5hdc into same sc, *skip 1sc, ss into next sc, 5hdc into same sc, rep from * to end.

Join side seams and sew armbands in place, matching seams and stitching row of sc to edge. Stitch braid in place.

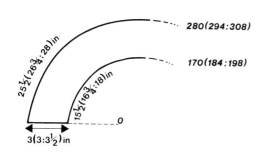

280(294:308)

170(184:198)

25½(26¾:28)in

15½(16¾:18)in

3(3:3½)in

0

Begin by putting 6[6:7] needles into holding position rep from row 6 to 31, 9 times more, then once to row 20[27:24]. Cast off.

On opposite side to cam box put 6[6:7] needles into holding position after rows 5, 7, 9 then bring 6[6:7] needles into working position after rows 11, 13, 15. Knit without shaping to row 31.

Beg with cam box on right [left:right], cast on 24[24:28] sts and work in st st to row 5[12:9].

Work second piece the same for Back.

**32in size only.** Cast off after row 121. 46 sts.
**34in size only.** Dec one st at each end after rows 129 and 130. Cast off after row 132. 50 sts.
**36in size only.** Dec one st at each end after rows 136, 137, 138, 139. Cast off after row 140. 54 sts.

Dec one st at each end after rows 66[74:81], 67[75:82], 68[76:83], 71[79:86], 72[80:87], 73[81:88], 76[84:91], 77[85:92], 78[86:93], 81[89:96], 82[90:97], 83[91:98], 86[94:101], 87[95:102], 88[96:103], 91[99:106], 92[100:107], 93[101:108], 96[104:111], 97[105:112], 98[106:113], 101[109:116], 102[110:117], 103[111:118], 106[114:121], 107[115:122], 108[116:123], 111[119:126], 112[120:127], 113[121:128], 116[124:131], 117[125:132], 118[126:133].

Inc one st at each end after rows 35[37:42], 39[42:47], 43[47:52], 47[52:57], 51[57:62], 55[62:67], 59[67:72], 63[72:77]. 112[120:128] sts. Knit without shaping to row 65[73:80].

Knit without shaping to row 35[37:42].

Cast on 96[104:112] and knit to row 33[36:39]. Drop every second stitch to pick it up on the WS with latchet tool, to make 1 by 1 rib.

## START HERE

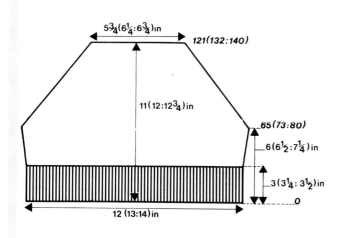

5¾(6¼:6¾)in

121(132:140)

11(12:12¾)in

65(73:80)

6(6½:7¼)in

3(3¼:3½)in

0

12 (13:14)in

1977

1978

# Crochet in circles

Worked as a circle, in four contrasting colors, this unusual 'cobweb' crochet weskit goes well over light blouses and tops.

## Size
Directions are for 34/36in bust.

### Gauge
4 sts and 2 rows to 1in over dc worked on No. G hook

## Materials
Coats & Clarks O.N.T. "Speed-Cro-Sheen" 100 yd. balls
3 balls main color A, brown
5 balls contrast color B, white
3 balls contrast color C, red
3 balls contrast color D, pink
One No. G (4.50 mm) crochet hook

## Main section

**NB** Garment is worked in one piece, beg at center back. Using No. G hook and A, ch6. Join with ss to first ch to form circle.

**1st round** Ch3 to count as first dc, 13dc into circle, join with ss to 3rd of 3ch. 14 sts.

**2nd round** Ch3 to count as first dc, 1dc into same place, 2dc into each dc to end, join with ss to 3rd of 3ch. 28 sts.

**3rd round** Ch3 to count as first dc, 1dc into same place, ch1, skip 1dc, *2dc into next dc, ch1, skip 1dc, rep from * to end, join with ss to 3rd of 3ch. 14grs of 2dc. Break off A and join in B to sp between first 2dc of round.

**4th round** Ch4, 1dc into same place, ch2, *(1dc, ch1, 1dc) between 2dc of gr, ch2, rep from * to end, join with ss to 3rd of 4ch.

**5th round** Ch4, 1dc between dc, ch3, *(1dc, ch1, 1dc) – called 1 gr – in ch1 sp of gr, ch3, rep from * to end, join with ss to 3rd of 4ch.

**6th round** Ch4, 1dc between dc, ch4, *1gr in ch1 sp, ch4, rep from * to end, join with ss to 3rd of 4ch.

**7th round** As 6th but working ch5 between gr instead of ch4.

**8th round** As 6th but working ch6 between gr.

**9th round** As 6th but working ch7 between gr. Break off B and attach C.

**10th round** Ch4, 1dc between dc, ch3, *1gr in ch7 loop, ch3, 1gr in ch1 sp, ch3, rep from * ending with 1 gr in ch7 loop, ch3, join with ss to 3rd of 4ch. 28grs.

**11th–14th rounds** As 6th–9th.
Break off C and attach D.

**15th round** As 10th. 56grs.
Break off D and attach B.

## Divide for armholes

**16th row** Ch4, 1dc between dc, ch4, *1gr in ch1 sp, ch4, rep from * 34 times more, 1gr in ch1 sp, turn, leaving 19grs unworked for back section.

**17th row** Ch4, 1dc between dc, ch5, *1gr in ch1 sp, ch5, rep from * 34 times more, 1gr in ch1 sp, turn.

**18th row** As 17th but working ch6 between gr.

**19th row** As 17th but working ch7 between gr.
Break off B and attach A.

**20th row** Ch4, 1dc between dc, ch3, *1gr in ch7 loop, ch3, 1gr in ch1 sp, ch3, rep from * skipping ch3 at end of last rep, turn.

**21st row** Ch4, 1dc between dc, ch3, *1gr in ch1 sp, ch3, rep from * skipping ch3 at end of last rep, turn. 73grs.

Rep 21st row 9 times more,

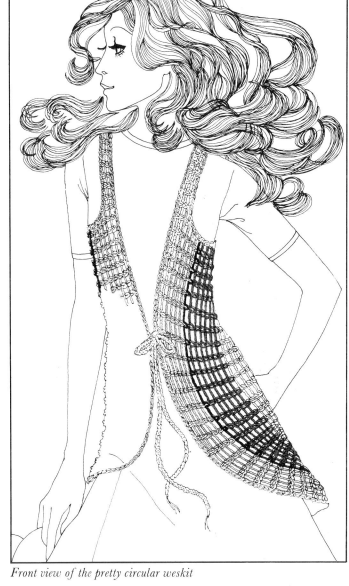

*Front view of the pretty circular weskit*

working 4 rows A, 1 row C and 4 rows D.

## Shoulder straps

Break off D and attach B.
**Next row** Ch36, into 5th ch from hook work 1dc, ch3, skip ch3, *1gr into next ch, ch3, skip ch3, rep from * 6 times more, work in patt to end of row, using a separate length of B, ch32 and fasten off yarn, return to main yarn and work across these 32ch with **skip ch3, ch3, 1gr in next ch, rep from ** to end, turn.
**Next row** As 21st, working across all sts including straps. Fasten off.

## Back section

Return to where 19gr were left, with RS facing skip

first 4grs, attach B and patt as given for 21st row across 11grs, turn and leave rem 4grs unworked.
Continue across these 11grs, rep 21st row 4 times more. Fasten off.

## Finishing

Join end of straps to each side of top of back section. Using No. G hook, B and with RS facing, work 1 row sc around all edges, easing in neckline and armholes to prevent fullness.
Press under a damp cloth with a warm iron.

### Lacing
Using No. G hook and 2 strands B, make a chain 20in long. Fasten off.
Thread lacing through edges at front waist to tie.

This piece of embroidery is really an essay on surface texture and light. The color of the work has been deliberately restricted to silver because the interest is achieved through reflective and padded surfaces. The play of light is extremely important and, according to the direction of the source of light, certain shapes come forward. Some appear dark and some light, giving the whole panel an interesting and effective range of silvery tones.

The restricted color of the panel also emphasizes the variety of surfaces in the embroidery: satin, crêpe, heavy weave, leather, plastic and vinyl. The threads receive particular attention for the same reason; some are tight and straight and others are used in heavy, lumpy lines of stitching.

The design for this embroidered panel was evolved from a drawing made of the end supporting frame of a weaving loom. When the drawing was slightly simplified, the designer found it related to a pattern in nine squares and this idea was emphasized. The vertical padded stripes originated from the slits through which the levers could be moved. The diagonal lines top left and right indicate the threads emanating from the loom and the horizontal base is the base of the loom.

In order to balance and make a design, lines and applied shapes have been added on the left and at the base of the panel. These give a circular flow around the vertical center which would otherwise be too dominant.